D0091296

Hot Chocolate

MICHAEL TURBACK

PHOTOGRAPHY BY LORI EANES

TEN SPEED PRESS
Berkeley | Toronto

Ten Speed Press
Box 7123
Berkeley, California 94707
www.tenspeed.com

Distributed in Australia by Simon and Schuster
Australia, in Canada by Ten Speed Press Canada,
in New Zealand by Southern Publishers Group,
in South Africa by Real Books, and in the
United Kingdom and Europe by Publishers
Group UK.

Photography by Lori Eanes
Cover and text design by Betsy Stromberg
Food styling by Randy Mon

"Double Chocolate Hot Chocolate" from
A Passion for Desserts by Emily Luchetti.
Copyright © 2003 Emily Luchetti. Used with
permission from Chronicle Books LLC, San
Francisco. Please visit www.ChronicleBooks.com.

"Chocolate Irish Coffee" from *Ghirardelli
Chocolate Cookbook* by the Ghirardelli Company.
Copyright © 1995 The Ghirardelli Company.
Used with permission from Ten Speed Press.

"Frrrozen Hot Chocolate" from *Sweet Serendipity*
by Stephen Bruce. Copyright © 2004 by Stephen
Bruce. Used with permission from Rizzoli International Publications, Inc.

Library of Congress Cataloging-in-
Publication Data
Turback, Michael.
  Hot chocolate / by Michael Turback.
      p. cm.
  Includes index.
  ISBN-13: 978-1-58008-708-7 (pbk.)
  ISBN-10: 1-58008-708-6 (pbk.)
  1. Chocolate drinks. I. Title.
  TX817.C4T87 2005
  641.6'374—dc22
                            2005010794
Printed in China

8 9 10 — 10 09 08 07 06

Contents

Acknowledgments vii

Introduction viii

Chocologue *Ingredients, Tools, and Techniques* 1

Sources and Origins *Ancestral Hot Chocolates* 13

Brave Old World *European Classics* 25

Haute Chocolate *Modern Variations* 36

For Adults Only *Spiked Hot Chocolates* 62

Second Childhood *Nostalgic Hot Chocolates* 85

Convivial Companions *Hot Chocolate Pairings* 105

Resources 138

Index 145

For Juliet, my sweet

Acknowledgments

Some things are destined to happen. At least that explains how this book seems to have hatched. The mysterious hand of fate brought together Dennis Hayes of Ten Speed Press and Maricel Presilla, culinary anthropologist/restaurateur, over enchanting after-dinner cups of hot chocolate at Zafra in Hoboken, New Jersey. The consequence of that evening is in your hands. I am grateful both to Dennis, for handing me an assignment any food writer would give his eyeteeth to land, and to Maricel, for encouraging and supporting my effort.

At the heart of this book are, of course, the inventive recipes, nearly every one developed by pastry chefs and chocolatiers specifically for this project. Thanks to every one of you for sharing a bit of your genius with the rest of us. My appreciation also goes to John Scharffenberger for helping me put the topic into proper perspective, and to Patricia Rain, David Lebovitz, Joe Calderone, Wendy Reisman, Stacy Cooper Dent, Leigh Merrigan, Martine Leventer, Philip Ruskin, Barbara Lang, and Jeffrey Turback, and to all the friends with whom I have so happily shared a cup. Here's mud in your eye! I am also deeply indebted to Lily Binns, my editor, and to Philip Aubrey Bobbs, my research assistant. Finally, I want to acknowledge the most important people in the life of this book—the readers. Thank you!

Introduction

The history books aren't certain about who first wrested nourishment from the cacao trees in the wilderness. Pods of the cacao tree, indigenous to the tropical Amazon rainforests, may have been harvested by the Olmecs, mother culture to the Maya, as early as 1000 B.C. But it was the remarkable Mayans themselves, rulers of what is now the Yucatan Peninsula in Mexico and Guatemala, who domesticated cacao, roasted and pounded its beans into a grainy, bitter paste, and placed the liquid at the center of their fantastic civilization.

While Europe slumbered in the Dark Ages, brilliant Mayan architects built elaborate temple-pyramids and ceremonial palaces, mathematicians mastered modular arithmetic, astronomers recorded the movements of the sun and moon to create the ancient world's most accurate calendar, and skilled farmers cleared large sections of the jungle for plantations of cacao trees without the advantage of metal tools or beasts of burden.

Eventually, Mayans shared their bounty with others living in cooler, drier highland regions unsuited to growing tropical cacao, and neighboring Aztecs depended on carriers who filled woven backpacks with beans to haul the precious cargo hundreds of miles on foot to their northern cities. Cacao was revered by the Aztecs, who combined it with spices to create a drink that was reserved for noblemen and warriors, and who exchanged the beans as currency. When Spanish conquistadors arrived to plunder the New World early in the sixteenth century, they discovered Aztec treasuries stockpiled not with silver or gold, but with cacao beans.

The curious notion of "money" growing on trees prompted the conquerors to enslave the so-called "Indians" and put them to work planting more cacao across South America and in Central America and islands in the Caribbean. But the new commodity and the bitter, spicy beverage that was made with it were not readily embraced back home in Spain, at least not until the more pungent spices in the drink were replaced with cane sugar and the drink was served hot instead of cold. With these refinements, and after nearly a century of exclusivity, Madrid became the center from which the liquid luxury spread across the entire continent.

Cacao became the jewel of European commerce, while chocolate beverages became fashionable among lords and ladies, poets and prelates. The upper classes sipped their steaming hot chocolate heavily sweetened and served in deep, straight-sided cups, while royalty flaunted their wealth by drinking from golden chalices. By the time the beverage made its way to the British Isles, milk had been added to the mixture, and although chocolate houses flourished in major cities, the price of drinking chocolate was out reach for the bourgeoisie.

In 1828, everything changed when a Dutch chemist developed a new way of pressing the fat from cacao beans. His method for creating cocoa powder made the drink more affordable and available to the masses, although the new drink paled in comparison to the original.

While most countries in Europe remained faithful to the more luxurious recipe, convenient cocoa powder prevailed in Britain and elsewhere. As those in the United States adopted the British fondness for cocoa, the drink seemed to lose its appeal among adults. Cocoa was relegated to adolescence and derided in literature as bedtime nourishment for schoolgirls. To make matters worse, Americans began using the terms "hot chocolate" and "hot cocoa" interchangeably, obscuring the considerable difference between the two.

True hot chocolate has maintained its exotic, romantic image in much of Europe, yet it has never been widely embraced on this side of the Atlantic. And while it's obvious that American temperaments are suited to the stimulation of coffee, a growing number of us long for a time when life was simpler and food was slower.

So, why on earth can't we make as decent a cup of hot chocolate as they do in Europe? How in heaven's name have so many of us missed out on experiencing the intense flavors, the rich and satisfying texture, and the unhurried ritual of melting fine chocolate and stirring it into warm milk? Restoring the seductive liquid to its rightful place in our culture is long overdue.

Hot chocolate is at once extravagant and familiar, provoking and comforting. It demands to be sipped slowly, savored as a treat that kindles feelings of safety and innocence while it gently lifts the spirits. Each cup offers refuge from the stresses of modern life, a change of pace from jam-packed schedules.

Between these covers is the fruit of my efforts to connect readers to a tradition that is several thousand years old. Here you will find recipes inspired by ancient ritual, traditional European classics, grandmotherly concoctions, and the imaginative inventions of preeminent pastry chefs and chocolatiers. It is my hope that no worthy hot chocolate has gone unstirred.

Michael Turback
Ithaca, New York

Chocologue

INGREDIENTS, TOOLS, AND TECHNIQUES

Just as American consumers have begun to enjoy more extravagant wines, beers, and coffees, so, too, are we beginning to appreciate the pleasures of real hot chocolate. This book is intended not only to demystify the process of preparing sophisticated drinking chocolates but also to advance the state of the chocolate arts with contributions from our most accomplished culinary virtuosos.

Before we begin talking about specific recipes and procedures, it's worth discussing what you'll need to have on hand. Although many ingredients on the following pages will be available at your local supermarket or gourmet food shop, consider stocking your cupboard with supplies that may be more difficult to find. As for equipment, hot chocolate requires few items other than what you probably already have in your kitchen.

INGREDIENTS

Master chocolatiers and pastry chefs take the same care in selecting chocolates as vintners do when choosing varieties to produce fine wines. Like the expression of *terroir* in wine grapes, it is interesting to see how cacao beans develop different characteristics when grown in different regions. Each high-quality chocolate contributes a distinctive aroma, personality, and complexity to the end result's final character. The most important principle when choosing chocolate for your drink, however, is to trust your own taste.

Chocolate

A package of fine chocolate will list the percent of cocoa butter and/or cacao solids it contains. High-quality chocolate contains more fat, which results in more flavor and a luxurious feeling on the tongue, or mouthfeel. The higher the number, the better the chocolate. Superior chocolates, the "couvertures" used by professional chefs, consist of 56 to 70 percent cacao solids and include 31 percent cocoa butter.

Unsweetened chocolate is pure chocolate liquor and about 50 percent cocoa butter. Bittersweet chocolate blends at least 35 percent liquor with as much as 50 percent cocoa butter, sugar, and vanilla. Semisweet chocolate has the same ingredients as bittersweet with the addition of more sugar. Milk chocolate, which contains about 10 percent chocolate liquor, takes the process a step further by adding about 12 percent milk solids. (Milk chocolate bars manufactured by Hershey's or Nestle's are eating chocolates, not cooking chocolates, and are not appropriate for these recipes.) Most of the recommended chocolates come in blocks and must be chopped or shaved so that they can be melted into hot chocolate.

> The divine drink, which builds up resistance and fights fatigue. A cup of this precious drink permits a man to walk for a whole day without food.
>
> EMPEROR MONTEZUMA
> OF THE AZTECS

Most of the recipes in this book call for dark, semisweet, or bittersweet chocolate, while a few use high-quality milk chocolate or white chocolate (since it does not contain cacao solids, white chocolate is technically not a chocolate). Where it makes a difference, the exact percentage of cacao or specific chocolate manufacturer is indicated.

See page 138 for top sources for chocolate.

Mexican Chocolate

Auténtico Mexican hot chocolate is made from a hockey puck–shaped tablet of bitter chocolate laced with cinnamon and covered in coarse sugar. Each tablet is divided into eight wedge-shaped segments that you can break off as needed. These rustic chocolates are available in Mexican markets, at some supermarkets, and from online merchants.

Shaved Chocolate/Hot Chocolate Mixes

Look upon the wide range of preshaved chocolates and prepared mixes as an invitation to experiment. Each version has its own individual aroma, personality, complexity, and composition. Not all drinking chocolate products are created equal, and they range from pure, 100 percent chocolate to mixes that include ingredients such as cocoa powder, cocoa butter, sugar, powdered milk, cornstarch, vanilla, and cayenne or other spices in addition to finely chopped bits of chocolate.

Cocoa Powder

Cocoa powder is made by extracting most of the rich cocoa butter from chocolate liquor (ground roasted cocoa beans) and pulverizing the dry residue. There are two types of cocoa powder: natural (nonalkalinized) and Dutch process (alkalinized). Natural cocoa powder (also called unsweetened) is simply untreated cocoa powder. Dutch process cocoa has been treated with an alkali to make the powder more soluble. Along the way, the "dutching" process gives the cocoa a deep mahogany color and a flavor reminiscent of Oreo cookies. The most popular American brands of cocoa

> Cocoa is a cad and coward; cocoa is a vulgar beast.
>
> G. K. CHESTERTON

powder contain about 7 percent cocoa butter, while specialty and European cocoa powders contain 12 to 24 percent cocoa butter. Some products contain cocoa powder alone, while others include artificial flavors, nonfat dry milk, preservatives, soy lecithin, vanilla, and sugar.

NOTE: In English-speaking countries, the word *cacao* came to be pronounced "cocoa," and *cocoa powder* is usually simply called "cocoa". As a result, most people assume that cocoa powder is just the ground beans themselves and that chocolate is made from cocoa powder instead of the other way around.

Spices

Spices, the dried roots, barks, berries, and other fruits of tropical seeds, were the earliest commodities to have driven global trade. These powerful, sensual aromatics have been used to impart their complex flavor to chocolates for thousands of years.

> So noble a confection, more than nectar & ambrosia, the true food of the gods.
>
> DR. JOSEPH BACHOT, 1662

For the best results, buy small quantities of ground spices and store them in tightly closed containers in a cool, dark, dry place for no longer than a year. Before using spices, sniff them. If their fragrance has diminished, toss them out. Chances are, the flavor has weakened as well and the spices will do nothing to improve your drink. If you're using nonsoluble spices in your hot chocolate, place them in a tea ball or wrap them in cheesecloth before dropping them into the liquid, so you can easily fish them out later.

Store vanilla beans completely submerged in granulated sugar. This method not only preserves the moisture and freshness of the beans but also creates an aromatic vanilla sugar that can be used for making cookies and other baked treats.

Sweeteners

Sugar is valuable not only for sweetening drinking chocolates but also for adding volume and tenderness and improving the drink's texture. Granulated white sugar, also known as table sugar, has medium-sized granules and is the sugar most often called for in recipes. When heated, granulated sugar takes on the color of toffee and a caramel flavor.

Confectioners' or powdered sugar, which has been crushed mechanically (and usually mixed with a little starch to keep it from clumping), is preferred in some recipes, especially iced chocolate drinks, because it dissolves more easily than granulated sugar.

Brown sugar is simply granulated white sugar with a bit of molasses to give it additional texture and color. Its color depends on the amount of molasses added during processing: the darker the color, the stronger the taste. Substituting brown sugar for white sugar in a hot chocolate recipe will add notes of butterscotch and molasses.

Sucanat is organically grown, freshly squeezed sugar cane juice that has been clarified, filtered, and evaporated. The syrup is then crystallized and granulated into sugar. Sucanat adds an extraordinary layer of caramel flavor to hot chocolate. It can be found in health food stores and some grocery stores.

> The superiority of chocolate, both for health and nourishment, will soon give it the same preference over tea and coffee in America which it has in Spain.
>
> THOMAS JEFFERSON

In Latin America, deeply flavored muscovado sugar (from the Spanish *mascabado,* meaning unrefined) is known as *rapadura, piloncillo,* or *chancaca.* The darkest of the raw dark brown sugars, muscovado has a fine-grained texture. Its natural molasses content results in a strong, lingering flavor that can't be matched by ordinary brown sugar. It marries well with the rich flavor of chocolate.

Conversions and Equivalents

FLUID MEASURES

10 ml = 2 teaspoons (t)	1 t = 5 ml
50 ml = 3 tablespoons (T)	1 T = 15 ml
100 ml = $3^1/2$ ounces	1 ounce = 30 ml
250 ml = 1 cup + 1 T	1 cup = 235 ml
500 ml = 1 pint + 2 T	1 quart = 950 ml
1 liter = 1 quart + 3 T	1 gallon = $3^3/4$ liters

DRY MEASURES

10 grams = $^1/3$ ounce	$^1/2$ ounce = 14 grams
50 grams = $1^3/4$ ounce	1 ounce = 28 grams
100 grams = $3^1/2$ ounces	$^1/4$ lb = 110 grams
250 grams = $8^3/4$ ounces	$^1/2$ lb = 230 grams
500 grams = 1 lb + $1^1/2$ ounces	1 lb = 450 grams

TOOLS

For Measuring

Solid chocolate is measured by weight (by the ounce) rather than by volume. Professional chocolatiers and pastry chefs use a scale to measure chocolate and other dry ingredients fast and accurately.

Digital and balance scales, which can be recalibrated to maintain their accuracy, are preferable to spring-loaded scales, which are not as precise and do not hold up as well over time. Home cooks can purchase inexpensive digital scales that hold up to six or seven pounds and are accurate to within $^1/8$ ounce; these scales also usually convert between grams and ounces.

To properly measure chocolate on most scales, first weigh the container that you are placing it in. Set the "zero" indicator at the container's weight. Then add the ingredients. In effect, you have ignored the weight of the container and only weighed the chocolate.

Chopping/Shaving

Most superior chocolate comes in blocks and must be either shaved using the large holes on a box grater or chopped into small pieces (about $1/8$ inch) with a knife before using. (Some manufacturers, however, are now making their chocolate available in small wafers or disks called pistoles, whose uniform size eliminates the need for chopping.)

Blocks of chocolate are easiest to work with at room temperature, when they can be chopped into pieces without splintering. To cut from the block the amount of chocolate you need, use a long serrated knife and score the block to a depth of about $1/8$ inch at the point you want to break it. Press the knife into the chocolate with firm, steady pressure at several spots along the scored line, advancing the knife a little deeper into the bar at each spot. Then, holding both the handle of the knife and the dull side of the blade, chop the block into small pieces that are as uniformly sized as possible, so that they will melt evenly. If the pieces are very different sizes, the chocolate won't melt evenly, and you run the risk of scorching the smaller pieces while you wait for the larger pieces to melt. To use a food processor instead of knife, chill the chocolate, bowl, and blade before pulsing the chocolate until chopped.

> The damnable agent of necromancers and sorcerers. It is well to abstain from chocolate in order to avoid the familiarity and company of a nation [Spain] so suspected of sorcery.
>
> FRENCH CLERIC, 1620

Melting/Cooking

One of the most popular methods for making hot chocolate is simply to stir small pieces of chocolate into hot milk in a nonreactive pan. (Substituting some of the milk with heavy cream results in a richer drink, while using some low-fat milk or adding some water allows more of the chocolate's subtle notes to come through.) Heat the milk over medium-low heat, removing the pan from the heat just before it reaches the boiling point. Overheating milk will destroy its flavor and mar its texture.

Ladle out a portion of the milk over the grated or shaved chocolate and stir with a wooden spoon until the mixture is well combined and forms a smooth paste. This base for the drink is called a ganache. Continue adding milk and gently stir until all the milk has been incorporated.

Let the chocolate "cook" in the milk while continuously stirring for a minute or two, then remove the mixture from the heat and allow the blended liquid to steep for ten minutes so its flavor fully develops. Return the hot chocolate to the heat and gently return it to a simmer before serving.

> Chocolate's properties are such that they stimulate love's ardour.
>
> LOUIS LEMERY,
> *TREATISE ON FOODS*, 1702

To retain the chocolate's full aroma, it should always be kept under a boil, and ideally its temperature should never exceed 180°F. An instant-read thermometer comes in handy for accurately gauging the temperature.

Always treat chocolate with respect in order to ensure the best result.

Mixing/Frothing

The more air you can get into the hot chocolate mixture, the frothier it will be. To impart a smooth, creamy texture to the drink, when the mixture begins to simmer, beat it vigorously with a wire whisk or fully submerge an immersion blender and whip until the surface of the drink is covered with foam. The best froth of all is made with the steamer of a cappuccino machine.

Purists, however, will argue that there is only one acceptable method for making frothy hot drinking chocolate. The *molinillo,* a carved wooden swizzle stick dating to seventeenth-century Spain, is the traditional tool of choice for whipping the liquid to form a frothy surface. As you twirl the stick between your hands, the round, flexible wooden base churns the chocolate. *Molinillos* can be found in Mexican grocery stores or purchased online.

Serving

The ancients drank chocolate from large bowls so they could take in all of its aromas. A deep bowl or mug continues to be the preferred method of serving lighter versions of the drink, while thicker, more concentrated hot chocolates are more sensibly served in demitasse or espresso cups. Warming the mug or cup before serving will slow the cooling of the drink.

Hot chocolate should be served with a spoon, which can be used for taking the first few sips of the piping hot beverage. If you're serving it to children, be sure it's not too hot for their palates, which are more tender than those of adults.

DARK SECRETS

Storing

To store chocolate, wrap it well, first in foil and then in plastic, and keep it cool and dry at temperatures between 60 and 65°F. Be sure to store it away from herbs, spices, and other aromatic foods, as it picks up other flavors relatively easily.

If stored under perfect conditions, dark chocolate actually improves with age, like a fine wine. Milk and white chocolate, on the other hand, should be stored for no longer than six to eight months. It is best not to refrigerate chocolate, and it should never be frozen.

The whitish color that can rise to the surface on chocolate is called fat bloom. It is caused by the cocoa butter separating due to fluctuations in the temperature. While it's not a pretty sight, bloom doesn't affect the chocolate's taste, and the cocoa butter will be redistributed throughout the chocolate when it is melted.

Resting

If you are patient, your hot chocolate will acquire wisdom and grace. Ideally, you should never drink hot chocolate immediately after making it, but rather you should let it rest and cool uncovered, then reheat it while stirring. When the mixture cools down, the chocolate crystallizes and the ingredients are bound together in a way that improves the drink's creamy, velvety texture.

> Hot chocolate must always be made from bars of chocolate, never from powder. Then it really becomes a noble product.
>
> MICHEL CLUIZEL, FRENCH CHOCOLATE MAKER

As far back as the eighteenth century, Madame d'Arestrel, superior of the Convent of the Visitation in Belley, France, instructed the epicure Jean-Anthelme Brillat-Savarin on the importance of letting hot chocolate rest: "When you would like to have some good chocolate, have it made the night before in a coffee pot and leave it. Resting overnight will concentrate it and give it a velvetiness that makes it even better. The good Lord cannot object to this little refinement, since He Himself is all excellence."

Note that most drinking chocolates can be made in advance and refrigerated for up to three days. To reheat, zap the liquid in a microwavable mug in short intervals, stirring well after each, until the mixture is hot.

Tasting

To maximize the pleasure of drinking chocolate, sip it slowly and allow the warm liquid to remain in your mouth for a few seconds to release its flavors and aromas. Nuances of high-quality dark chocolates are often compared to flower blossoms, smoke, earth scents, or teas. Take in the fragrance, crispness, intensity, concentration, and persistence of flavor. Enjoy the lingering taste in your mouth.

> We shall advise our fair readers to be in a particular manner careful how they meddle with romances, chocolates, novels, and the like inflamers, which look upon as very dangerous to be made use of.
>
> *BRITISH SPECTATOR, 1905*

Taste preferences change with the seasons, not only because we mentally associate hot chocolate with cold weather but also because our bodies need to generate more heat in colder conditions. Hot chocolate also provides the increased calories that our bodies need for energy to combat the elements.

The Pleasure Principle

Drinking chocolate's reputation for stirring the senses has been a subject of discussion for centuries, from the Emperor Montezuma, who fortified himself with chocolate before entering his harem, to Madame de Pompadour, who relied on hot chocolate to warm her passion for Louis XV. Chocolate, it seems, releases phenylethylamine—the same chemical released by the body during moments of love and arousal—into the system, causing a rise in blood pressure, increasing the heart rate, and inducing feelings of well-being that borders on euphoria. This once-mysterious phenomenon explains chocolate's mood-elevating and libido-enhancing effect.

Health Benefits

In 1662, renowned English physician Dr. Henry Stubbe recorded that one cup of chocolate contained more fat and nourishment than a pound of meat, and he began writing medical prescriptions for chocolate. He insisted that chocolate could restore energy after a day of hard labor, alleviate lung inflammation, and strengthen the heart.

Dr. Stubbe may have been on to something. In 1998, Dr. Chang Yong Lee and colleagues at Cornell's Department of Food Science and Technology in Geneva, New York, carried out tests to compare antioxidant levels in red wine and hot chocolate. The study found that a cup of hot chocolate was twice as rich in antioxidants as a glass of red wine, which these days is touted by many as beneficial to the heart. Antioxidants—which include vitamins C and E and beta carotene—are widely believed to fight cancer, heart disease, and aging. Part of the secret to the antioxidant magic is the "hot" in hot chocolate. Apparently, heat releases more of the antioxidants into the beverage.

> T'will make old women young and fresh, create new motions of the flesh and cause them long for you know what. If they but taste of chocolate.
>
> JAMES WADWORTH,
> *A HISTORY OF THE NATURE AND QUALITY OF CHOCOLATE*

Sources and Origins

ANCESTRAL HOT CHOCOLATES

SPICES OF ANTIQUITY

Sweet Spice-Scented Hot Chocolate   15

Pungent Spice-Infused Hot Chocolate   16

Hellfire Hot Chocolate   17

THE MESTIZO LEGACY

Life-in-a-Cup Hot Chocolate   19

Nueva Bogotá Hot Chocolate   21

Chocolate Caliente para Agasajos   23

Long ago, civilizations learned to collect, store, dry, roast, and grind cacao to form a basic chocolate paste, and this paste, when mixed with water and agitated, made a frothy, rather bitter stimulant. To temper its bitter character, Mesoamerican women devised cocktails made with the fragrant buds, berries, roots, and seeds they collected from the tropical rainforests. Each tribe, partial to a distinctive combination of spices, fresh herbs, and nuts, had its own essential blend. Each new ingredient added not only its unique flavor but also its distinctive warming or cooling properties to create an entirely new taste poem.

SPICES OF ANTIQUITY

Once you understand the history of drinking chocolate, re-creating the varieties enjoyed during antiquity can be taken in many directions. The more extreme approach would involve using indigenous ingredients and, whenever possible, primitive techniques. Another method, and a far more practical one, is to adapt ancient recipes to modern tastes, choosing ingredients to suit your individual preferences.

Combining chocolate and spices is the art of the possible. Success comes from blending compatible but contrasting flavors, body (textures), and basic taste sensations. This is a highly subjective, inexact endeavor. Use the recipes that follow as guideposts, but also use your sense of taste, and trust your own instincts. Smell each ingredient as you add it and be conscious of the contribution each is making to the final result. When you sip the hot liquid, consider the spices you've added and see if you recognize them. When you have a basic understanding of the various spices and how they have complemented the drink throughout history, you can use your own creativity and instincts to create unlimited combinations.

Sweet Spice-Scented Hot Chocolate

Drinking chocolate reaches the height of sophistication with the addition of vanilla. This sensuously supple spice is obtained from tropical pods that grow on fragrant climbing orchids; the pods are cut from the vine while green, then cured by sweating under blankets until they turn black. The native Mexican vanilla bean is thicker and darker than other beans, with a more powerful fragrance and deeper flavor. Indigenous vanilla used for thousands of years in this region is the richest and most satisfying. Vanilla beans should be plump and pliable and feel dense and somewhat oily. The longer the bean, the better the flavor. To use a vanilla bean to flavor milk for hot chocolate, cut the bean in half, split it lengthwise with a knife, scrape the seeds into the liquid, and throw in the pod as well. The tiny seeds and pulp of the vanilla bean have the most flavor, but the pod will impart a certain complexity.

1 cup whole milk

1 vanilla bean

4 ounces bittersweet chocolate, finely chopped

1 teaspoon confectioners' sugar

Combine the milk and vanilla bean in a small saucepan over low heat. Simmer for 10 minutes. Remove the bean. Add the chocolate and stir continuously with a wooden spoon until completely melted. Add the sugar and stir until combined. Remove the mixture from the heat and allow to steep for 10 minutes. Return to the stove over low heat and gently return to a simmer before serving.

MAKES 1 SERVING

Chocolate and the King are my only passions.

QUEEN MARIA THERESA OF SPAIN

Pungent Spice-Infused Hot Chocolate

Hot chocolate provides the perfect canvas for spices such as cinnamon and cloves, whose heady aromas will unfold in layers as you sip this drink. The bark of the cassia tree, which grows abundantly in tropical America, is the source of *canela*, or what we call cinnamon. It has a sweet, orangelike, and balsamy fragrance and a distinct, robust flavor that nips the tongue. Cinnamon quills are made from long pieces of bark that are rolled, pressed, and dried. They make great stirrers for hot chocolate, although the quills are often rolled so tightly that it's difficult to get much flavor out of them. If this is the case, give them a whack with a blunt instrument. They'll break into pieces, releasing more of their essence. If you don't have any cinnamon quills on hand, ground cinnamon can be substituted.

Cloves are the dried, unopened buds of a tropical evergreen tree. They have a penetrating, warm, sweet flavor and an alluring, almost hypnotic aroma. They can be used either whole or ground; when used whole, they must be removed before serving.

1 cup whole milk

1 cinnamon quill or 1 teaspoon ground cinnamon

2 whole cloves or $1/2$ teaspoon ground cloves

4 ounces bittersweet chocolate, finely chopped

1 teaspoon confectioners' sugar

Combine the milk with the cinnamon and cloves in a small saucepan over low heat. Simmer very slowly for 10 minutes. Remove the cinnamon quills and whole cloves. Add the chocolate and stir continuously with a wooden spoon until completely melted. Add the sugar and stir until dissolved. Remove the mixture from the heat and allow to steep for 10 minutes. Return to the stove over low heat and gently return to a simmer before serving.

MAKES 1 SERVING

Hellfire Hot Chocolate

Of the thousands of concoctions that slide down throats in the name of hot chocolate, the most fascinating is, without question, the fierce, bitter brew spiked with hot pepper.

Cayenne, the dried fruit of a pepper plant native to the tropics, was well known by ancient civilizations who regularly seasoned chocolate drinks with the orange-red powder. When cayenne is eaten, the capsaicin in it stimulates the release of endorphins to quiet the pain caused by the burning sensation, many believe. The more cayenne consumed, the more endorphins generated by the brain. As a side effect, the endorphins produce a pleasant euphoria. The ancients no doubt became addicted to the cycle of pain and pleasure, since records show they reached for the succor of chocolate several times a day.

Allspice is the pea-size berry of the evergreen pimiento tree, also native to Central and South America. Allspice gets its name because it tastes like a combination of cinnamon, nutmeg, and cloves. In this recipe, allspice contributes complex spice flavors to balance the heat in the fiery hot chocolate.

1 cup whole milk

1/4 teaspoon ground cayenne pepper

1 teaspoon ground allspice

4 ounces bittersweet chocolate, finely chopped

1 teaspoon confectioners' sugar

Combine the milk, cayenne, and allspice in a small saucepan and heat slowly to just under a boil, about 5 minutes. Add the chocolate and stir continuously with a wooden spoon until completely melted. Add the sugar and stir until dissolved. Remove the mixture from the heat and allow to steep for 10 minutes. Return to the stove over low heat and gently return to a simmer before serving. Serve immediately.

MAKES 1 SERVING

THE MESTIZO LEGACY

The term *mestizo* has come to identify people of mixed European and Latin American Indian racial descent, or, in a broader sense, to describe the blending together of the two cultures. After the conquest of the Americas and during the colonial period, indigenous cuisine changed dramatically. Spanish missionaries who landed in Mexico with the conquistadors were not only active in evangelizing the natives, they were responsible for the intermingling of cuisines.

Cacao and the drink derived from the precious beans first made their way to Europe through a network of monasteries and convents. Once it was made more palatable to the Europeans by warming and sweetening, a slow fusion of the two culinary cultures was inevitable. *Mestizo* recipes for hot chocolate have been arousing passionate emotions ever since.

Before drinking their beloved chocolate, Latin American Indians poured the warm liquid back and forth from cup to pot until it developed a thick head of dark foam called *espuma*. They believed the spirit of the drink was in the froth's meditative glow. If the chocolate didn't have *espuma*, it wasn't alive. Not satisfied with the ancient method of agitating chocolate, Spanish colonists invented an intricately carved wooden whisklike tool called a *molinillo* that is twirled back and forth between the palms of the hands, like a Boy Scout starts a fire, until froth is produced, inhibiting the formation of the skin that can develop on top of the drink. In some villages, a woman's culinary skill was judged by the thickness of her foam—the taller the lather, the better the cook. And a bride might prepare a chocolate drink with a cap of foam and offer it to her groom as a part of the marriage ritual.

Life-in-a-Cup Hot Chocolate

Jan Purdy, Señor Fred, Sherman Oaks, California

You might say that life begins and ends with chocolate in the diverse indigenous communities of the southern Mexican state of Oaxaca. When a Oaxacan child is born, parents invite friends and relatives to share bowls of chocolate. At communions, weddings, and anniversaries, too, hot chocolate is at the center of the celebration. And at the end of life, the dead are buried with tablets of native chocolate.

For this recipe, pastry chef Jan Purdy was inspired by Oaxacan *champurrado*, its *mestizo* ancestor. She updated it with bittersweet chocolate, masa meal for texture, and brown sugar, which adds a molasses flavor. She places the cup on a plate surrounded by a variety of home-made Mexican cookies.

2 1/4 cups whole milk

3/4 cup heavy cream

6 ounces bittersweet chocolate, chopped

1/2 teaspoon ground cinnamon

2 tablespoons masa meal

1/4 cup firmly packed brown sugar

Basic whipped cream for serving (page 137)

Ground cinnamon for serving

Combine the milk and cream in a small saucepan and bring to a simmer over low heat. Whisk in the chocolate until completely melted. Add the cinnamon, masa meal, and brown sugar. Stir constantly until slightly thickened, 2 to 3 minutes. Working in batches (hot liquids will expand in the blender), transfer to a blender and process until smooth. Serve immediately, or refrigerate until ready to serve and reheat each serving in the microwave until steaming hot, 3 to 4 minutes. Adjust the thickness, if desired, by adding a little milk or water, and top with whipped cream and a sprinkle of cinnamon.

MAKES 6 DEMITASSE SERVINGS

Nueva Bogotá Hot Chocolate

Michael Antonorsi, Chuao Chocolatier, Encinitas, California

It's hard to imagine a more honestly rendered drinking chocolate than this one devised by Michael Antonorsi, inspired by his fond memories of his childhood in Bogotá, Colombia. "My home was in the Andes at an altitude of 2,600 meters (8,500 feet), and it was cold at night even in the summer," he says, recalling the energetic hot chocolates served at family gatherings. In his powerfully flavorful homage to *mestizo* tradition, the rich chocolate displays fruity undertones that blend with exuberant spices, resulting in soul-satisfying complexity.

Cheese is added to Colombian hot chocolates the same way we add marshmallows to ours. Cut the cheese into small cubes and add it to the chocolate immediately before serving. The result is a chewy, salty sensation that heightens anticipation for the next sip of sweetness. You can use any type of cheese that will not dissolve when exposed to heat but will hold together and get chewy inside, such as Colombian *queso blanco*, Mexican *queso panella*, Greek *hilloumi*, or anything else used for grilling or frying.

NOTE: *Papelon, panela, pilonzillo,* and *panocha*—types of raw sugar rich with molasses—can be found in Latin American markets, they come in solid blocks and can be grated with a cheese grater.

2 cups whole milk

4 ounces Venezuelan bittersweet chocolate (58.5 percent cacao), chopped

2 tablespoons grated papelon, panela, pilonzillo, panocha, or firmly packed brown sugar

Pinch of ground cardamom

Pinch of ground chipotle chile

1/2 pinch ground cayenne pepper

1/2 pinch salt

2 ounces white farmer's cheese or other grilling cheese

CONTINUED

In a small saucepan, heat the milk over medium-low heat to just under a boil. Place the chocolate, sweetener, cardamom, chipotle chile, cayenne, and salt in a separate small saucepan. Pour about 1 cup of the hot milk over the chocolate and stir until the chocolate is melted and smooth. Stir in the remaining cup of milk.

Place the chocolate mixture over medium heat and cook, stirring constantly, until hot but nowhere near boiling. Cut the cheese into 1/4-inch cubes. Pour the chocolate into cups and top with cubes of cheese. Serve immediately.

MAKES 2 SERVINGS

Fruit of all the kinds that the country produced were laid before him; he ate very little, but from time to time a liquor prepared from cocoa, and of an aphrodisiac nature, as we were told, was presented to him in golden cups. . . . I observed a number of jars, above fifty, brought in, filled with foaming chocolate, of which he took some.

BERNAL DIAZ DEL CASTILLO, MEMBER OF CORTEZ'S FORCE,
DESCRIBING A MEAL OF EMPEROR MONTEZUMA, 1519

Chocolate Caliente para Agasajos

Maricel Presilla, Zafra, Cucharamama, Hoboken, New Jersey

In seventeenth-century Spanish colonial cities of Mexico, elegant afternoon soirées called *agasajos* centered on the drinking of hot aromatic chocolate. Served to female guests along with marzipan, nougats, and cold drinks, the frothy hot chocolate was flavored with aromatic spices like anise, vanilla, rosebuds, and even hot peppers. Not unlike the heady cacao drinks the Spanish conquistadors found in Mesoamerica, seventeenth-century chocolate was colored with either reddish achiote seeds, an indigenous coloring, or with Spanish saffron.

In this re-creation by Maricel Presilla, America's leading Latina culinary scholar, saffron is used for a more emphatic Spanish taste. She also suggests using fine chocolate made with a single variety of Venezuelan cacao beans or a blend containing a high percentage of Venezuelan beans, since beans from Venezuela were the choice for most aristocratic households in Spain and the colonies. Her interpretation of this historic drinking chocolate is a vibrant vestige of another age, a journey to a world that seems strange and wonderful. NOTE: Rosebuds are available in Middle Eastern shops and also in Latin American markets, where they are sold as *rosa de Castilla*.

8 cups whole milk

1/4 ounce rosebuds

2 teaspoons lightly crushed saffron

3 three-inch Ceylon cinnamon quills

1 tablespoon ground aniseed

1 dried hot chile (such as árbol or piquín)

1/2 cup sugar

2 plump Mexican vanilla beans

7 ounces bittersweet chocolate (60 percent to 70 percent cacao), coarsely chopped

Combine the milk, rosebuds, saffron, cinnamon, aniseed, chile, and sugar in a

CONTINUED

nonreactive 6-quart saucepan and bring to a boil over medium heat. Split the vanilla beans in half lengthwise, scrape out the seeds with a small knife, and add both seeds and beans to the milk mixture. Lower the heat to medium-low and simmer for 10 minutes. Remove from the heat and let sit, covered, for 10 minutes more. Strain the mixture into another saucepan and return to a gentle simmer over medium heat. Stir in the chocolate and beat vigorously with a wire whisk or a Mexican *molinillo* until you have raised a bubbly froth. Serve piping hot.

VARIATION: For a richer, more full-bodied drink, increase the quantity of chocolate to 10 ounces.

MAKES 8 SERVINGS

Montezuma took no other beverage than the *chocolatl,* a potation of chocolate, flavored with vanilla and spices, and so prepared as to be reduced to a froth the consistency of honey, which gradually dissolved in the mouth and was taken cold.

WILLIAM HICKLING PRESCOTT,
THE HISTORY OF THE CONQUEST OF MEXICO, 1838

Brave Old World

EUROPEAN CLASSICS

Heisse Schokolade mit Schlagobers   27

Het Choklad Vit   28

Chocolate a la Taza   30

Cioccolato Caldo   31

Hot Chocolate   32

Heisse Schokolade mit Mélange   33

Le Chocolat l'Africain   35

When Anne of Austria, a Hapsburg-Spanish princess, married Louis XIII of France in 1615, wedding gifts to her betrothed included an ornate casket of chocolate—along with a maidservant to prepare the chocolate for drinking. You can almost imagine the king, wrapping his hands around a magnificent goblet of thick, steaming chocolate with spices from far-flung corners of the world.

Hot chocolate continues to enjoy a princely reputation in the cities of Europe, from cozy bistros to elegant cafés in the grand tradition. Over the centuries, these inspiring cafés have provided a taste of monarchial luxury to the masses. With an oh-so-civilized hot chocolate made from exquisite chocolate bars melted into cream, served in style, and savored at length, you can't help but view the world as a better place.

> If you are not feeling well, if you have not slept, chocolate will revive you.
>
> MARQUISE DE SÉVIGNÉ

Heisse Schokolade mit Schlagobers

Café Mozart, Vienna, Austria

Vienna's immortal Café Mozart, which opened just three years after the legendary composer's death in 1791, has always been a place where people come to stay warm. For the price of a cup of coffee or hot chocolate, you can linger for hours. Café Mozart's ornate wood-paneled dining room, and its sidewalk tables in warm months, are the city's best destination for hot chocolate accompanied by a variety of cakes and strudels. Five different versions of the drink are made with Venezuelan chocolate and served in china cups under the watchful eye of the *ober* (headwaiter). And whipped cream is not an option, but a must.

Heisse Schokolade with *schlagobers* (whipped cream) is the standard portion, while *Oma's Schokohäferl,* or grandmother's hot chocolate, arrives in a cup twice as large. The most popular hot chocolates are spiked with amaretto, Cointreau, or, in the case of *Wiener Schokolade,* the café's specialty, rum.

3 ounces bittersweet chocolate, chopped
1 ounce unsweetened chocolate, chopped
1 teaspoon confectioners' sugar
Pinch of salt
1 cup whole milk
1/2 teaspoon pure vanilla extract
Basic whipped cream for serving (page 137)

In the bowl of a food processor fitted with a metal blade, combine the chocolates, sugar, and salt. Process on high just until the chocolates are finely ground. In a medium saucepan, heat the milk over medium-low heat to just under a boil. Add the chopped chocolate mixture and continue cooking, stirring constantly, until the mixture thickens slightly, about 5 minutes. Remove from the heat and whisk in the vanilla. Pour into a china cup, top with softly whipped cream, and serve immediately.

MAKES 1 SERVING

Het Choklad Vit Chokladkoppen, Stockholm, Sweden

On the vibrant main square of Stockholm's old town (Stortorget), outdoor cafés provide blankets and serve steaming hot chocolate so patrons can still enjoy the street scene when days grow shorter and the weather chillier. Although only six years old, the cozy café called Chokladkoppen (The Chocolate Cup) feels like it's been here for a century. Small, handmade tables and chairs are provided for natives and tourists who come for the city's best hot chocolate, topped with a froth of steamed milk, served in ceramic cups and bowls, and accompanied by gargantuan cinnamon rolls.

If you're looking for something to take the chill off the six-month-long Scandinavian winter, look no further than Chokladkoppen and its creamy, silky-smooth Hot White Chocolate.

1 cup whole milk

4 ounces Valrhona Ivoire White Chocolate, chopped

1 teaspoon pure vanilla extract

1 orange slice

In a medium saucepan, heat the milk over medium-low heat until very hot but not boiling. Gradually add the white chocolate to the hot milk, stirring constantly with a wooden spoon until the chocolate is melted and the mixture is smooth. Stir in the vanilla. Remove from the heat and froth with a steamer or immersion blender. Pour into a mug and arrange the orange slice as a garnish. Serve immediately.

MAKES 1 SERVING

Chocolate a la Taza Chocolatería San Ginés, Madrid, Spain

It has been said that Madrileños rarely sleep. Restaurants, nightclubs, and cafés in their city bustle until the wee hours of the morning, regardless of the day of the week. But once the bars close, sweet-seekers converge on Chocolatería San Ginés for *churros y chocolate*—spirals of deep-fried dough coated in sugar and cinnamon, and served with a thick, chocolate pudding–like drink for dunking—that mark the traditional end to a night out.

Drinking chocolate, having stood the test of time for nearly four centuries, is taken very seriously by the Spaniards. Warm, melted chocolate, scented with vanilla and sweetened separately with sugar, has been a supreme joy at San Ginés since 1894. In the happy chaos of five o'clock in the morning, night owls crowd around marble-topped tables for the local breakfast ritual of people-watching while dipping *churros* into the thickest hot chocolate imaginable.

$^{1}/_{2}$ cup whole milk
$^{1}/_{4}$ cup heavy cream
4 ounces semisweet chocolate, chopped
$^{1}/_{2}$ teaspoon cornstarch
$^{1}/_{2}$ teaspoon pure vanilla extract

In a saucepan, combine the milk and cream and heat over medium-low heat until very hot but not boiling. Gradually add the chocolate to the hot liquid, stirring constantly with a wooden spoon until the chocolate is completely melted and the mixture is smooth. In a small cup, dissolve the cornstarch in a few tablespoons of water. Add the dissolved cornstarch to the chocolate mixture and stir constantly until it is almost as thick as a pudding. Serve immediately in warmed cups.

MAKES 2 DEMITASSE SERVINGS

Cioccolato Caldo Caffè Florian, Venice, Italy

Open since 1720 and set under the arcades of the Procuratie Nuove in Piazza San Marco, Caffè Florian is the spiritual home of Italian hot chocolate. Here two 25-liter containers "cook" the blend of Costa Rican chocolates and milk for up to five hours. The secret of the molten, deliquescent chocolate is the long, slow cooking period, plus the addition of cornstarch, which adds body to the rich drink. Waiters in starched white jackets serve the drink in tall glasses with silver holders, the bottom half filled with the thick, viscous liquid, the top half with fresh whipped cream.

4 ounces bittersweet chocolate, chopped
1 cup whole milk
1/4 teaspoon cornstarch
Basic whipped cream for serving (page 137)

Place the chocolate in a saucepan. In a separate saucepan, heat the milk over medium-low heat to just under a boil.

Gradually pour 1/4 cup of the milk onto the chocolate, stirring constantly so that it melts evenly and no lumps are formed. When you have a creamy paste, add the remaining milk and stir until combined. In a small cup, dissolve the cornstarch in a few tablespoons of water. Add the dissolved cornstarch to the chocolate mixture and stir constantly until the liquid thickens. Return the saucepan to the stove and cook over low heat, stirring frequently with a wooden spoon to avoid sticking or burning, until a creamy film forms on the sides of the saucepan, about 20 minutes. The longer you heat the mixture, the creamier the drink will be. If it begins to boil, remove the pan from the heat and place it on a cool, heatproof surface, such as steel or marble, to lower the temperature. Once it has cooled slightly, return it to the heat. Pour into a tall glass and fill to the top with softly whipped cream.

MAKES 1 SERVING

Hot Chocolate
L'Artisan du Chocolat, London, England

When it comes to hot chocolate, Gerard Coleman is a classicist, and he has an almost whispering reverence for a properly made cup. He uses 70 percent Brazilian couverture with fruity, woody, and almond flavors that are intensified when the chocolate is heated. He believes that to achieve a smooth texture, hot chocolate must be prepared like a mayonnaise, the ingredients carefully combined to ensure a proper emulsion.

At L'Artisan du Chocolat, hot chocolate is served from an urn filled with rich liquid that has thickened and whose flavors have been allowed to concentrate during a resting period. According to Gerard, one should never drink hot chocolate immediately, but rather let it rest and cool uncovered, then reheat. He suggests preparing it the night before, then drinking it with breakfast. "If you must have it straight away," says Gerard, "make a double batch, one for here and now, and one for the following day, when you'll enjoy it even more."

3/4 cup whole milk

1/4 cup heavy cream

2 tablespoons firmly packed brown sugar

Pinch of salt

Dash of pure vanilla extract

4 ounces bittersweet chocolate, chopped

In a small saucepan over medium-low heat, combine the milk, cream, brown sugar, salt, and vanilla and heat until it measures about 176°F on a candy thermometer. Put the chocolate into a small bowl. When the milk has reached the proper temperature, carefully pour 1/4 cup of the hot milk into the chocolate. Stir constantly, using small circular moves in the center (as you would for a mayonnaise), until it forms a shiny paste. Pour the paste back into the remaining hot milk mixture and stir until thoroughly blended. Let it cool uncovered. Pour through a fine-mesh sieve into a clean saucepan and gently reheat over low heat. Serve immediately.

MAKES 2 DEMITASSE SERVINGS

Heisse Schokolade mit Mélange

Grand Restaurant Schuh, Interlaken, Switzerland

Despite Switzerland's reputation for confections, chocolate did not arrive there until fairly recently, and since the Swiss believed the substance to be a medicine, it was only sold in apothecaries. By the mid-nineteenth century, however, chocolate had become fashionable, and *schokoladestuben,* or chocolate houses, started appearing on the landscape.

In 1886, Christian Schuh opened a café in the center of Interlaken, where up to three hundred patrons could view the snow-capped Alps through large windows. In a large dining room set with cheerful pink tablecloths, guests are serenaded by a pianist while feasting on tea and pastries or on hot chocolate, the centerpiece of sociability and a cherished ritual at Grand Restaurant Schuh.

In Swiss tradition, the café makes its own chocolate from choice South American beans. Bittersweet couvertures are grated and melted into milk, and the result is served with softly whipped cream

(mélange). Waiters suggest *Schwarzwälder Kirschtorte,* the café's specialty Black Forest cake, as the perfect accompaniment.

1 cup whole milk

4 ounces semisweet chocolate, shaved

1 teaspoon confectioners' sugar

Basic whipped cream for serving (page 137)

In a saucepan, heat the milk over medium-low heat until it reaches a simmer. Add the chocolate and sugar, and stir with a wooden spoon until the chocolate has melted and the mixture reaches the desired consistency. Remove from the heat and allow to steep for 10 minutes. When ready to serve, gently reheat over low heat, pour into a warmed cup, top with whipped cream, and serve immediately.

MAKES 1 SERVING

Le Chocolat l'Africain
Angelina, Paris, France

For centuries, the French have attributed amazing properties to hot chocolate. The last queen of France, Marie Antoinette, employed a personal chocolatier from Vienna to concoct hot chocolate mixed with powdered orchid bulbs for breakfast, with orange blossoms to soothe a sore throat, and with almond milk to settle an upset stomach.

In 1903, Antoine Rumpelmayer opened the doors to a grand café on the Rue de Rivoli, which he named for his beloved daughter-in-law, Angelina. Although her elegance has faded somewhat, the grand dame remains a popular destination for solvent tourists who don't mind waiting in line to sip the famous thick brew as they bear witness to a bygone age. Aromatic chocolate from African estates provides the base for Angelina's Le Chocolat l'Africain. Poured from a steaming pot into a porcelain cup and delivered with a ramekin of whipped cream on the side, the drink is described by the French newspaper *Le Monde* as "lethally delicious."

3/4 cup whole milk

1/4 cup heavy cream

1 teaspoon confectioners' sugar, or to taste

4 ounces Omanhene bittersweet chocolate (72 percent cacao), chopped

Basic whipped cream for serving (page 137)

In a small saucepan over medium-high heat, combine the milk, cream, and sugar and heat just until bubbles appear around the edges of the pan. Remove the pan from the heat and add the chocolate, stirring with a wooden spoon until it is completely melted. If necessary, return the pan to low heat, stirring constantly, until the chocolate is melted. The mixture should appear smooth and evenly colored. Serve warm (not hot) in demitasse or espresso cups with softly whipped cream on the side.

MAKES 2 DEMITASSE SERVINGS

Haute Chocolate

MODERN VARIATIONS

Tarragon and Black Pepper Hot Chocolate   38

Chinese Five-Spice Hot Chocolate   40

Double Chocolate Hot Chocolate   42

Hungarian Heat   43

Citrus Hot Chocolate   44

Café-Style Hot Chocolate   45

Lavender-Pistachio Hot Chocolate   47

Peppermint Hot Chocolate   48

Scharffen Berger Hot Chocolate   49

La Bonne Table Hot Chocolate   50

Bay Leaf–Infused Hot Chocolate   52

Caramel Hot Chocolate   54

Ginger-Caramel Hot Chocolate   56

Matcha Hot Chocolate   58

Peanut Butter Hot Chocolate   59

Malted Hot Chocolate   60

It took the ingenuity of cloistered monks to adapt the Aztec recipe to suit the Spanish palate, and it was their skill with chocolate that is responsible for the drink's rise to reverence. With the benefit of pharmaceutical training, the Jesuits not only perfected a technique for roasting and grinding cacao beans, they also replaced the drink's harsh spices with cane sugar and, in a giant leap for mankind, they first served it hot, releasing its full aroma and complex chocolate essence. Monasteries were entrusted with keeping the secrets of this newfound luxury for the benefit of Spain, and drinking chocolates remained a well-kept secret from the rest of Europe for almost a hundred years.

Today's high priests of hot chocolate, our estimable pastry chefs and chocolatiers, make no secret of their own passion for experimentation. Their modern variations—harmonious blends of rich flavors and velvety textures—provide a glimpse into the future of drinking chocolates.

Tarragon and Black Pepper Hot Chocolate

Jenn Stone, JS Bonbons, Toronto, Canada

As a young girl, Jenn Stone remembers not being allowed to drink coffee with the grown-ups. "Chocolatey cocoa was our pacifying hot drink," she recalls. "Hot chocolate's connection to our childhood is why we think of it as comfort food."

Inspired by her shop's edgy menu of truffles and guided by her instincts as a former pastry chef, Jenn anoints a base of Valrhona chocolate with the aniselike essence from dark-green leaves of fresh tarragon and the woody, piney kick of black pepper. Heat intensifies the flavor of both spices, so expect a bold, assertive hot chocolate. While it might provoke youthful memories, this sophisticated drink is definitely for the mature palate.

NOTE: Black pepper loses its flavor quickly, so for the most penetrating aroma use freshly ground pepper both in the ganache and as a finishing touch over the whipped cream.

GANACHE

1 bunch fresh tarragon, washed

3 cups heavy cream

1 teaspoon sea salt

2 tablespoons freshly ground black pepper, plus more for serving

3 tablespoons unsalted butter

15 ounces bittersweet chocolate, finely chopped

HOT CHOCOLATE

4 cups 2 percent milk

Basic whipped cream for serving (page 137)

To make the ganache, combine the tarragon and cream in a saucepan and bring to a boil over medium-low heat. Add the salt and pepper, then remove from the heat. Let the mixture steep until the cream has fully absorbed the tarragon and pepper flavors, about 2 hours.

Return the mixture to medium-low heat and bring to just under a boil. Add the butter and stir to combine. Put the chocolate into a heatproof bowl and strain the cream mixture through a fine-mesh sieve onto the chocolate. Stir until completely smooth, then strain again into a clean, dry container. This ganache can be stored in the refrigerator for up to 5 weeks.

To finish the hot chocolate, place the ganache in the top part of a double boiler. Fill the bottom pan with no more than an inch of water, making sure not to let it touch the top pan. Heat the water and ganache over very low heat, making sure the water does not boil. Once the ganache is warm (not hot), transfer it to a small saucepan and combine with an equal portion of milk. Stir over medium heat until well combined. Top with whipped cream and a hint of coarsely ground black pepper and serve immediately.

MAKES 8 TO 10 SERVINGS

The beverage prepared from these chocolate cakes was very rich in butter, and whilst the British Navy has always consumed it in this condition, it is a little heavy for less hardy digestions.

ARTHUR W. KNAPP, *COCOA AND CHOCOLATE*, 1920

Chinese Five-Spice Hot Chocolate

Christopher Elbow, Christopher Elbow Artisanal Chocolate, Kansas City, Missouri

Young Christopher Elbow was introduced to European-style hot chocolate during his high school French club's visit to Paris. Breakfasts there, including croissants and "an eat-it-with-a-spoon, thick, rich hot chocolate," were the earliest influences on his career as pastry chef.

In his postmodern chocolate chop in Kansas City, Christopher embellishes truffles with calligraphy-style brushstrokes and Jackson Pollock–esque splatters. His artistic interpretation of drinking chocolate employs a pungent, aromatic mixture of Asian spices to transform the beverage into a modern masterpiece. NOTE: A staple of Chinese cooking, pre-mixed five-spice powder is available in Asian markets and many supermarkets.

1 star anise
1/2 teaspoon fennel seed
1 cinnamon quill
6 whole cloves
10 whole Szechuan peppers
4 cups whole milk
16 ounces semisweet chocolate, chopped
Basic whipped cream for serving (page 137)
Ground cinnamon for serving

In a saucepan over medium heat, combine the anise, fennel, cinnamon, cloves, peppers, and milk and bring to a simmer. Remove from the heat and let steep for 5 minutes. Strain through a fine-mesh sieve to remove the spices and return the milk to the saucepan over medium-low heat. Stir in the chopped chocolate until melted completely. Bring to a slow simmer and whisk for 30 seconds. Pour the hot chocolate into warm mugs and top with freshly whipped cream and a sprinkle of cinnamon. Serve immediately.

MAKES 4 SERVINGS

Double Chocolate Hot Chocolate

Emily Luchetti, Farallon, San Francisco, California

The hot chocolate that Emily Luchetti remembers drinking while she was growing up in New York's Finger Lakes region was always accompanied by lots of marshmallows. "You couldn't put them all in at the beginning," she recalls. "You had a bowl on the side, so after the marshmallows were all gone, you got to reload."

Emily's recipe combines dark chocolate, milk chocolate, and cocoa powder for a caressing texture and depth of flavor without overwhelming the palate. She serves her effortlessly charming hot chocolate in small demitasse cups with a pitcher standing by for refills.

1 1/3 cups heavy cream
1 1/2 cups whole milk
11 ounces dark chocolate, finely chopped
5 ounces milk chocolate, finely chopped
3 tablespoons unsweetened cocoa powder
Pinch of salt

In a saucepan, warm the cream and milk over medium heat, stirring frequently, until hot and bubbling around the edges. Remove the pan from the heat and add the chocolates, cocoa powder, and salt. Let sit for 15 seconds, then whisk until smooth. Pour into espresso or demitasse cups and serve immediately, or let cool and store, covered, in the refrigerator. When ready to serve, reheat in the microwave or a double boiler until hot.

MAKES 6 DEMITASSE SERVINGS

Hungarian Heat

Joanne Mogridge, Cocoa West Chocolatier, Bowen Island,
British Columbia, Canada

Bowen Island is a 20-square-mile chunk of rock lying two miles off the west coast of Canada. It is home to three thousand people, three mountains, two valleys, four lakes, two species of salmon, and one charming chocolate shop called Cocoa West, where artisan chocolate maker Joanne Mogridge practices her craft. When Joanne's brother returned from Hungary with some of the country's prized air-dried paprika, Joanne turned it into spicy-hot truffles that, in turn, inspired a fearless hot chocolate with intense flavor and distinctive heat.

Hot paprika is made from the whole pepper, ground seeds and all, instead of just the pod, and its spiciness explodes in the warm liquid. Serve with a small glass of room temperature water to cleanse the palate.

4 cups 2 percent organic milk
1 teaspoon finely ground Hungarian hot paprika
$1/2$ teaspoon finely ground white pepper
2 whole cloves
7 ounces organic semisweet chocolate (56 percent cacao), chopped

In a saucepan over medium-low heat, combine the milk, paprika, pepper, and cloves and heat until almost boiling. Remove the cloves. Decrease the heat to low and add the chocolate, stirring with a wooden spoon until completely melted. Whisk to a generous froth, pour into warmed cups, and serve immediately.

MAKES 4 SERVINGS

Citrus Hot Chocolate

Patrick Coston, The Art of Chocolate, New York, New York

Pastry chef Patrick Coston has spent years refining the art of sweet indulgences. His fresh treatment of hot chocolate finds a middle ground between overindulgence and understatement. The citrus oil flavoring is clear and strong, yet it doesn't overwhelm the taste of the chocolate. Instead, it adds an aromatic expression and cuts some of the richness, while giving the mouth a comparison point. A final touch of luxurious Grand Marnier liqueur lends flavors of orange, spice, and vanilla to the masterwork.

2 oranges

1/4 cup sugar

3 cups heavy cream

1 cup whole milk

12 ounces bittersweet chocolate (65 to 80 percent cacao), chopped

2 tablespoons Grand Marnier

8 orange slices

Basic whipped cream for serving (page 137)

Using a box grater, remove the zest from the oranges, being careful not to grate down to the bitter white pith. Combine the zest and sugar in the bowl of a food processor fitted with a metal blade and process until the oils are released from the zest, 1 to 2 minutes. Place the orange sugar in a large saucepan with the cream and milk and bring to a simmer over medium-low heat. When the mixture reaches a simmer, turn off the heat and add the chopped chocolate. Whisk well until smooth and the chocolate is completely melted. Add the Grand Marnier and whisk well. Strain the hot chocolate through a fine-mesh sieve, divide among demitasse cups, and top with an orange slice and whipped cream.

MAKES 8 DEMITASSE SERVINGS

Café-Style Hot Chocolate

Jacqui Pressinger, Patisserie Bleu, Nashua, New Hampshire

"All it takes is the aroma of hot chocolate to trigger memories of snow, snowsuits, snowball fights, and growing up in chilly New Hampshire winters," says Jacqui Pressinger. According to Jacqui, when you are bringing heavy cream to a simmer to make a ganache for your hot chocolate, it's the perfect time to steep in extra flavors. This is achieved by adding chunks of crystallized ginger, or, for that matter, fresh mint leaves, dried lavender, or even washed banana skins. Just be careful to strain these items out of the cream completely before adding the chocolate.

In addition to being used as the base for hot chocolate, this ganache can also be used as a glaze for cakes or as a hot fudge sauce. It will stay fresh in the refrigerator for up to 2 weeks in a sealed container.

GANACHE

1 cup heavy cream

2 tablespoons light corn syrup

10 ounces dark chocolate (58 percent cacao)

HOT CHOCOLATE

1/2 cup boiling water

1/2 cup whole milk, steamed, frothed, or heated

To make the ganache, in a saucepan over medium-low heat, combine the cream and corn syrup and heat until it reaches a simmer. Turn off the heat and stir in all of the chocolate until completely melted.

To make the hot chocolate, place hot or room temperature ganache in a bowl and slowly pour the boiling water on top. Stir until combined. Stir in the milk and serve immediately.

MAKES 2 SERVINGS

Lavender-Pistachio Hot Chocolate

Robert Kingsbury, Kingsbury Chocolates, Alexandria, Virginia

Rob Kingsbury's modern lavender libation is decidedly perfumed and slightly musky, the lavender adding an intriguing dimension to the warm chocolate. Used in aromatherapy to comfort and soothe the tired body and mind, lavender conveys its tranquility-inducing and relaxation-inducing properties to this drink.

Rob uses culinary lavender imported from Provence, available at gourmet food shops. The darker the color of the blossom, the more intense the flavor. Use it sparingly at first, then add more as needed. Placing the lavender in a mesh tea ball is a convenient way to infuse its flavor into the milk, since it can easily be removed after steeping, but if you do not have a tea infuser, simply toss the loose lavender buds into the hot milk and remove with a fine-mesh sieve.

Pistachios are more than just a garnish here. The roasted and salted nuts add an alluring savory note to complement the liquid chocolate.

2^1/$_2$ cups whole milk

4 teaspoons lavender

12 ounces shaved bittersweet chocolate

Basic whipped cream for serving (page 137)

4 tablespoons chopped roasted salted pistachios

In a medium saucepan, bring the milk to a simmer over medium-low heat. Turn off the heat, cover the pan, add the lavender, and steep in the hot milk for 3 to 5 minutes. (The longer you leave the lavender in the milk, the stronger its flavor will be.) Remove the tea infuser of lavender, if using, or strain the milk through a fine-mesh sieve. Add the chocolate to the warm milk and whisk vigorously until the chocolate is melted and the mixture froths. Pour equal amounts into 4 mugs, top each with a dollop of whipped cream, and sprinkle with chopped pistachios.

MAKES 4 SERVINGS

Peppermint Hot Chocolate

Ethan Howard, Martini House, St. Helena, California

Pastry chef Ethan Howard created this fanciful cup of cheer to accompany a dessert of assorted gingerbread confections called "Santa's Cookie Plate." His peppermint concoction is the essence of the holiday season, but you can make it any time of the year.

Although peppermint oil is used extensively to flavor confections, its therapeutic qualities shouldn't be overlooked. If you overindulge in a meal, a small cup of Ethan's peppermint-boosted hot chocolate is a sensible and enjoyable way of helping along your digestion. In fact, that's why mint-flavored candies and liqueurs are often taken after dinner. At Christmastime, the emotional pull is strong, and peppermint hot chocolate delivers inner warmth along with shared memories.

2 cups whole milk

1 cup heavy cream

2 tablespoons pure vanilla extract

1 1/2 cups sugar

16 ounces bittersweet chocolate, chopped

2 teaspoons salt

1/2 teaspoon peppermint oil

Combine the milk, cream, vanilla, and sugar in a saucepan over medium heat. When the mixture is hot, add the chocolate and stir constantly until the hot chocolate is completely melted. Continue stirring while adding the salt and peppermint oil. When the mixture reaches a simmer, remove it from the heat and serve immediately.

MAKES 6 DEMITASSE SERVINGS

Scharffen Berger Hot Chocolate

John Scharffenberger, Scharffen Berger Chocolate, Berkeley California

Chocolate can be as rich and interesting as wine, according to John Scharffenberger, a California vintner for fifteen years before becoming an artisan chocolate maker. Indeed, aficionados often describe premium dark chocolate in wine-making terms: as oaky, acidic, woodsy, smoky, fruity, or citrus-scented. John retains a winemaker's sensibility in the blending of beans, most grown on small farms of less than five acres, from growers in Sulawesi, Panama, Venezuela, Madagascar, and Ghana. He roasts each variety separately, grinds them, then blends them together to achieve the company's signature flavor.

Comparing hot cocoa to hot chocolate, he points out that the most significant difference is in viscosity. "When you're drinking real hot chocolate, you're drinking whole, pure chocolate, so you're getting cocoa butter," says John. "With the butter comes a lot of the high notes of chocolate, the perfumey, fruity notes, and more luscious, deeper flavors."

His recipe is so rich that he suggests serving an espresso- or a double espresso–size portion.

6 ounces Scharffen Berger bittersweet chocolate (70 percent cacao)
1 quart milk or half-and-half

Break the chocolate into small pieces and place in a small, heavy saucepan. Add 1 cup of the milk and melt over medium-low heat while stirring constantly. When the chocolate has melted, increase the heat to medium and add the remainder of the milk while whisking rapidly. Do not allow the mixture to come to boil. Reduce heat and simmer for five minutes. Pour into cups and serve immediately.

MAKES 6 TO 8 SERVINGS

La Bonne Table Hot Chocolate

Victor Béguin, La Bonne Table, Peterborough, New Hampshire

Victor Béguin insists that melting chunks of dark chocolate is the best and most authentic way to make hot chocolate. The flavorful version of the drink he serves at La Bonne Table depends on a unique natural sweetener called Sucanat, developed thirty years ago by his Swiss uncle, Dr. Max-Henri Béguin. "Hot chocolate and Sucanat are a perfect match," says Victor, "and a historical match." Somewhat similar to unrefined sugars used for thousands of years, Sucanat (the word is condensed from "sugarcane natural") is made by crushing sugarcane to squeeze out the juice, then concentrating it into a thick, rich syrup that is simply dehydrated and milled into a powder.

"It is not only healthier than white sugar, but it also dissolves easily and lends the drink a creamy caramel taste," says Victor, who also suggests putting a pinch of sea salt into hot chocolate. "It seems like a little thing to add, but salt really helps to bring out a richness in the chocolate, in the same way it improves fudge." Finally, he borrows from his knowledge of Indian Brahman cooking with the addition of a dash of cardamom or saffron—in his words, "two of the most sublime flavors in the world," and both known as aids to digestion. NOTE: Sucanat is available in most health food and organic grocery stores.

1 gallon whole milk

1 vanilla bean or 1 teaspoon pure vanilla extract

1 cup semisweet chocolate, chopped, or to taste

1 cup Sucanat, or to taste

Pinch of sea salt

Pinch of ground cardamom or saffron

In a saucepan, bring the milk to a simmer over medium-low heat. If using a vanilla bean, cut the bean in half, scrape out the seeds, and add the bean and the seeds to the milk as it heats. Add the chocolate and Sucanat and whisk to blend. Taste and add more Sucanat or chocolate, if desired. Stir in the salt and cardamom. If using vanilla extract, add it now. If using a vanilla bean, remove it from the hot chocolate, and serve immediately.

MAKES 16 SERVINGS

If any man has drunk a little too deeply from the cup of physical pleasure; if he has spent too much time at his desk that should have been spent asleep; if his fine spirits have become temporarily dulled; if he finds the air too damp, the minutes too slow, and the atmosphere too heavy to withstand; if he is obsessed by a fixed idea which bars him from any freedom of thought: if he is any of these poor creatures, we say, let him be given a good pint of amber-flavored chocolate . . . and he will experience a marvel.

JEAN-ANTHELME BRILLAT-SAVARIN

Bay Leaf–Infused Hot Chocolate

Sisha Ortuzar, 'wichcraft, New York, New York

Sisha Ortuzar's hot chocolate, served to go in 12-ounce paper cups, has attracted raves from *New York Magazine*. Its secret ingredient is the leaf of the bay tree, an ancient herb native to the Mediterranean region. In fact, it was a garland of bay leaves that rewarded victors in battle and sporting events in early Greece and Rome. The chef suggests using fresh bay leaves whenever possible. The very intense flavor of the fresh herb tends to mellow when dried for a few days. If you can't find fresh bay leaves, crinkle the dry leaf just before using to release the pungent, spicy fragrance that is the herb's signature.

The drink is neither cloyingly sweet nor is it too rich. "My hot chocolate is meant to be lighter than some recipes," says Sisha, "so you can actually manage to finish the entire cup." At the restaurant, he recommends enjoying it with *pain perdu* (French toast), a scone, or their signature cream'wich cookie.

GANACHE

9 ounces bittersweet chocolate (61 percent cacao), chopped

1 cup heavy cream

HOT CHOCOLATE

6 cups whole milk

1 large or 2 small fresh bay leaves, or more as needed

2 cups ganache

To make the ganache, cut the chocolate into small pieces and place in a heat-proof bowl. In a saucepan, bring the cream to a gentle boil over medium-low heat. Remove from the heat and slowly pour a small amount over the chocolate, stirring with a rubber spatula. Wait until the cream is incorporated before adding more. When all the cream is added, the chocolate will be melted and the ganache should be smooth. You can make the hot chocolate now, or you can allow the ganache to cool and store, covered, in the refrigerator, for up to 24 hours.

To make the hot chocolate, combine the milk and bay leaf in a saucepan and bring to a simmer over medium-low heat. Taste it; the bay leaf flavor should not overpower but it should impart a nice aroma. If necessary, add another bay leaf or allow the mixture to steep while simmering until it achieves the desired flavor. Add the ganache and whisk until it dissolves completely and the mixture returns to a simmer. Pour the hot chocolate through a fine-mesh sieve to strain out the bay leaves and serve immediately.

MAKES 6 SERVINGS

LET THEM DRINK CHOCOLATE

After being found guilty of treason by the French Revolutionary Tribunal, Marie Antoinette retired to her cell for a supper of roast chicken. Then, at 7 A.M., when it was time to prepare for the guillotine, she asked for a cup of chocolate along with a pastry, which was brought in from a neighboring café.

Caramel Hot Chocolate

Fran Bigelow, Fran's Chocolates, Seattle, Washington

One of the more persuasive ways to indulge nostalgic taste buds is by drinking this creation by Fran Bigelow, master artisanal chocolatier and owner of Fran's Chocolates, a shop that has achieved cult status among chocolate lovers in Seattle. She has a reputation for using the best sweet ingredients to enhance chocolate flavors, not overwhelm them, just as she does with the caprice of caramel enveloped in warm, sumptuous chocolate.

This recipe achieves "a wonderful marriage of my two favorite flavors," says Fran. "The hot milk releases the flavor and sensuality of the chocolate, while caramelizing the sugar provides a depth of flavor and a long, lingering finish." She suggests gilding the lily by topping the hot chocolate with whipped cream, then drizzling it with additional caramel sauce.

CARAMEL SAUCE

1 1/4 cup sugar
1/4 cup water
3/4 cup heavy cream

HOT CHOCOLATE

5/8 cup whole milk
1 1/2 ounces bittersweet chocolate (65 percent cacao), thinly shaved or grated

To make the caramel sauce, combine the sugar and water in a saucepan over medium heat. Cook, stirring occasionally, until the sugar is dissolved and the mixture is clear. Increase the heat to high and bring to a boil. Cook, without stirring, until the mixture turns a light golden brown, about 10 minutes. Occasionally brush down the sides of the pan with a pastry brush dipped in water. When the mixture begins to caramelize and brown around the edges, and has the distinct, nutty fragrance of caramel, lift and gently swirl the pan to encourage even browning.

When the caramel is a deep golden brown, remove from the heat and slowly pour in the cream, continuously stirring with a long-handled wooden spoon. The sugar will bubble up vigorously as the steam escapes. Keep stirring until the bubbling stops and the mixture is smooth. Let cool about 15 minutes. Store in a sealed container in the refrigerator for up to 2 weeks.

To make the hot chocolate, in a small saucepan, bring the milk to a simmer over medium-low heat. Remove from the heat and stir in the chocolate until completely smooth, about 1 minute. Stir in 2 tablespoons of the caramel sauce and serve immediately.

MAKES 1 SERVING

I've been stirring for half an hour now;
The chocolate is finished, and there's nothing left for me
But the smell and an empty mouth.
Isn't my mouth like yours?
Oh mistresses, why should you get the real thing and I only the smell of it?
By Bacchus, I'm going to taste it. Oh, it's good.

LORENZO DA PONTE, LIBRETTO FOR *COSÌ FAN TUTTE* BY MOZART

Ginger-Caramel Hot Chocolate

Kimberly Davis Cuthbert, Sweet Jazmine's, Berwyn, Pennsylvania

Contemporary hot chocolates often flirt with a combination of both childhood and adult flavor preferences. One of the most compelling examples of this phenomenon is this creation by pastry chef Kimberly Davis Cuthbert, which relies on the pixielike contrast of caramel and ginger.

As a child, Kim drank hot chocolates either overflowing with marshmallows or piled high with whipped cream. Her grown-up version of hot chocolate fuses the sweet heat of fresh ginger with the buttery, smoky notes of slightly burnt caramel, adding double "bite" to the dreamy dark chocolate.

CARAMEL SAUCE

1 cup heavy cream

1/2 cup unsalted butter

3 fluid ounces corn syrup

2 cups sugar

HOT CHOCOLATE

3 cups whole milk

1 cup heavy cream

6 ounces bittersweet dark chocolate (58 percent cacao), chopped

1 heaping tablespoon minced fresh ginger

To make the caramel sauce, in a saucepan over high heat, combine the cream and butter and heat until melted together. Remove from the heat, but cover to keep warm.

In a separate saucepan over medium-high heat, heat the corn syrup until it constantly bubbles on the surface, about 1 minute. Slowly add the sugar about 1/2 cup at a time, waiting a few minutes between each addition. Every time more sugar is added the mixture will take on a deeper amber color. Once all of the sugar is melted, leave the saucepan on the heat and stir constantly until the sugar gets a bit darker, to golden brown, and just starts to vaporize a little. When white pockets in the sugar start to bubble, remove the sugar from the heat.

Wearing oven mitts to protect yourself from burns caused by the steam that's created, very carefully add the cream and butter mixture in three parts, stirring well after each addition. Once all of the liquid has been added, keep stirring until the bubbles have subsided. The caramel is still very hot, so be careful not to touch it. At this stage add it to the cocoa mixture.

To make the hot chocolate, combine the milk, cream, chocolate, ginger, and $3/4$ cup of the caramel sauce in a saucepan over low heat. Allow this combination to melt the chocolate and steep the flavors of the caramel and ginger. Keep on the heat for 20 minutes, stirring constantly, until ready to serve.

MAKES 4 SERVINGS

If one swallows a cup of chocolate only three hours after a copious lunch, everything will be perfectly digested and there will still be room for dinner.

JEAN-ANTHEME BRILLAT-SAVARIN

Matcha Hot Chocolate

Greg Hook, Chocolate Arts, Vancouver, British Columbia, Canada

One of Vancouver's most distinguished pastry chefs, Greg Hook, explores the sensory possibilities of the hot chocolate cuppa, balancing white chocolate with jade-green matcha, the powdered tea leaves served in a Japanese tea ceremony. Upon harvest, tea leaves are steamed, dried, and slowly ground with a stone mill into very fine powder to produce exotic matcha, whose well-developed scent, intense flavor, and vivid color become the soul of this beverage. Borrowing from the Zen of the ancient ceremony, the essence of the matcha is at one with the white chocolate.

1 cup half-and-half

1 teaspoon matcha powder

4 ounces white chocolate, finely chopped or grated

In a heavy saucepan over medium heat, warm the half-and-half, stirring often to prevent sticking, until it is very hot. Remove from the heat and sprinkle in the matcha and then the white chocolate. Allow white chocolate to melt, about 1 minute. Using an immersion blender, mix until thoroughly combined and the liquid is frothy. Pour into serving cups and serve immediately.

VARIATION: Milk can be substituted for the half-and-half, although it will need to be stirred more often to prevent it from sticking to the pan.

MAKES 2 DEMITASSE SERVINGS

Peanut Butter Hot Chocolate

Scott Campbell, @SQC Restaurant & Bar, New York, New York

There are those who love winter, and there are those who cope better in winter with hot chocolate.

"Hot chocolate isn't just for kids anymore," says Scott Campbell, chef and owner of @SQC on Manhattan's Upper West Side, who has created an entire family of hot chocolates that are served all day long in bathtub-size cups at the bar at @SQC. The kinetic maestro has created a tantalizing collision of warm chocolate and salty peanut butter, combining two favorite candy bar flavors to evoke memories of childhood safety and comfort.

1 quart whole milk

3/4 cup unsweetened cocoa powder

1/4 cup sugar

6 ounces bittersweet chocolate, chopped

2 ounces light corn syrup

5 ounces organic peanut butter

Homemade marshmallows for serving (optional; page 132)

Basic whipped cream for serving (optional; page 137)

Combine the milk and cocoa powder in a saucepan over medium-low heat and bring to a simmer. Add the sugar. Reduce the heat to low and add chocolate, stirring occasionally until melted, 3 to 5 minutes. Meanwhile, in a bowl, stir together the corn syrup with the peanut butter until very smooth. Stir the peanut butter mixture into the hot chocolate and strain through a fine-mesh sieve. Pour into serving cups, top with homemade marshmallows or whipped cream, if desired, and serve immediately.

MAKES 4 SERVINGS

Malted Hot Chocolate

Matt Lewis, Chocolate Bar, New York, New York

The hip, pocket-size West Village shop called the Chocolate Bar stocks a signature line of nostalgia-influenced chocolate bars. It comes as no surprise that New Yorkers go gaga over creamy, dreamy liquefied candy bars, so the shop also serves a variety of drinking chocolates as an alternative beverage to over-caffeinated city dwellers. This cross between a thick, rich malted milk shake and steaming, velvet hot chocolate is perhaps the most retro.

Malted Hot Chocolate is served with just a smidgeon of humor, in bowls, not cups, that are filled half-full so there's lots of room to stick your nose inside—and to inhale the aromas. With the first sip, you taste the chocolate, and with the second, you notice the familiar flavor of malt.

3 ounces bittersweet chocolate, chopped
1/4 cup boiling water
1/4 cup heavy cream
1/4 cup skim milk

1 1/2 tablespoons malted milk powder
Basic whipped cream for serving (page 137)
Crushed malted milk balls for serving

Place the chocolate in a small heatproof bowl. Pour the boiling water over the chocolate, making sure all the pieces are submerged. Set aside for about 3 minutes. While waiting for the chocolate to melt, combine the cream and skim milk in a saucepan and bring to a simmer over medium-low heat. Stir in the malted milk powder. Whisk the chocolate and water mixture until smooth, then pour immediately into the milk and cream mixture. Whisking constantly, bring the mixture just to a boil. Divide the hot chocolate among 2 mugs and top with whipped cream. Sprinkle crushed malted milk balls over the whipped cream and serve immediately.

MAKES 2 SERVINGS

For Adults Only

SPIKED HOT CHOCOLATES

Samuel Adams Adult Hot Chocolate   65

Hot Chocolate Buttered Rum   66

Mocha Voodoo   68

Hot Chocolate Reviver   69

Roasted Hazelnut Hot Chocolate   70

Sake-Wasabi Hot Chocolate with Tahini Cookies   72

Maple-Whiskey Chocolate Hot Toddy   75

Hot Chocolate Nightcap Tequila   76

Midnight Cowboy   77

Brown Russian   79

Chestnut Hot Chocolate   81

Hot Chocolate à l'Orange   82

Chocolate Irish Coffee   84

Chocolate and alcohol have been conjoined throughout history. The Incas mixed a corn-based beer with drinking chocolate, and their Spanish conquerors diluted it with wine. Antonin Carême, the French pastry maestro who cooked for Napoleon, the king of England, and the tzar of Russia, improved the drink even further with the addition of luxurious ingredients like cognac and fresh cream. Early American gentlefolk depended on hot drinks to combat spiritually challenging winters and unheated homes. While the fireplaces of taverns may have provided the best place to warm up on the outside, bartenders spiked belly-warming cocoas along with grogs, nogs, and flips to do their work on the inside.

Of course, as humorist Ogden Nash's saying goes, "Candy is dandy, but liquor is quicker." When bone-chilling cold rages outside, comfort comes in the form of a spiked hot chocolate sliding down the hatch. This well-worn remedy has stood the test of time.

Samuel Adams Adult Hot Chocolate

Boston Beer Company, Boston, Massachusetts

Cream stout is traditionally the richest and sweetest of the stouts, which makes it pair more graciously with drinking chocolate than you would have thought possible. The chile powder in this drink brings out the chocolate and beer flavors without adding too much heat. The first sip of this beautiful brunette liquid goes down with a kick of chile and a pleasant, smoky aftertaste that lingers on the palate. On the second sip, the moderate bitterness of the hops is balanced by the creamy chocolate and rich brown sugar flavors.

NOTE: Use the best semisweet (not bittersweet) chocolate possible.

2 (12-ounce) bottles Samuel Adams Cream Stout
6 tablespoons firmly packed brown sugar
Lemon wedge to rim the glasses
Granulated sugar to rim the glasses
4 ounces semisweet chocolate, chopped
$1/2$ teaspoon chile powder
White chocolate for shaving (optional)

Warm 4 martini glasses by filling them with hot water and letting them sit while you make the hot chocolate. To make the hot chocolate, in a saucepan over medium-low heat, combine the beer and brown sugar and bring to a gentle boil, cooking for about 3 minutes. While the chocolate is cooking, pour the water out of the martini glasses, run the lemon wedge around the rims of the glasses, and dip the rims into a saucer of granulated sugar until the desired amount of sugar has collected on the glass. Reduce the heat under the saucepan to low and whisk in the chocolate and chile powder. Pour into the warmed sugar-rimmed martini glasses. Garnish with white chocolate shavings, if desired, and serve immediately.

MAKES 4 SERVINGS

Hot Chocolate Buttered Rum

Michelle Gayer-Nicholson, Franklin Street Bakery, Minneapolis, Minnesota

Rum has been a prominent ingredient in warm drinks ever since the days when Britain's Royal Navy ruled the seas, and hot buttered rum is a tradition dating back to the days when Americans were British subjects. In an inspired fusion of two classic winter drinks, Michelle Gayer-Nicholson of the Franklin Street Bakery in Minneapolis captures the scents of chocolate, full-flavored dark rum, maple syrup, sultry spices, and vanilla cream. The result is quite aromatically happy.

Sip this fragrant potion by the fireside with good friends all around. It will make your toes tingle. It's also an excellent remedy for anyone coming down with anything.

COMPOUND BUTTER

2/3 cup unsalted butter, at room temperature
1/8 cup unsweetened cocoa powder
3/4 cup firmly packed brown sugar

MASCARPONE CREAM

1 (8-ounce) tub mascarpone
1 vanilla bean

HOT CHOCOLATE

3 cups half-and-half
Zest of 1 orange
1/4 teaspoon ground nutmeg
1/4 teaspoon ground cinnamon
1/4 cup maple syrup
2 pinches of salt
3 1/2 ounces bittersweet chocolate, chopped
3 ounces dark rum

To make the compound butter, using a stand mixer fitted with the paddle attachment, cream the butter, cocoa powder, and brown sugar until smooth, scraping down the sides of the bowl as needed with a rubber spatula. Place the mixture in a pastry bag fitted with a star tip. Pipe rosettes the size of a silver dollar onto a parchment-lined baking sheet and place in the freezer until ready to serve. The unused portions can be sealed in an airtight container and frozen for up to 1 month.

Cut the vanilla bean in half lengthwise and scrape out the seeds with the tip of a knife. Add the seeds to the mascarpone in the bowl of a stand mixer fitted with the whisk attachment. Whip until the mascarpone forms soft peaks, scraping down the sides of the bowl as needed with a rubber spatula. Cover and refrigerate until ready to use.

To make the hot chocolate, in a saucepan over medium-low heat, combine the half-and-half, orange zest, nutmeg, cinnamon, maple syrup, and salt and bring to a low boil. Remove from the heat and allow to steep for 15 minutes. Return the mixture to a simmer over low heat, add the chocolate, and whisk vigorously until fully melted. Remove from heat.

To assemble the drink, pour 1 ounce of dark rum in each of three glasses. Add 1 piece of compound butter to each glass and pour the hot chocolate on top. Spoon a dollop of the vanilla mascarpone cream on top and serve immediately.

MAKES 3 SERVINGS

Mocha Voodoo

Mary Sonnier, Gabrielle, New Orleans, Louisiana

Mary Sonnier's eccentric hot chocolate is an evocation worthy of New Orleans's legendary voodoo priestess, Marie Laveau. But the potion has more to do with the restaurant Gabrielle's contemporary Creole cuisine, characterized by enchanting complexity, bold tastes, and unusual combinations, than with the casting of spells or keeping the bayou spirits at bay.

Chicory, the roasted ground root of Belgian endive, is often served in a duet with coffee in New Orleans. This assertive chicory-laced coffee blended with chocolate and spiced rum is calculated to warm the body and soul. Sprinkle cayenne on top, and think of it as voodoo dust.

2 cups half-and-half

6 ounces semisweet chocolate, chopped

1/2 cup spiced rum, such as Captain Morgan's

2 tablespoons sugar

2 cups strong brewed coffee with chicory, or espresso

Basic whipped cream for serving (page 137)

Ground cayenne pepper for serving

In a 3-quart saucepan with tall sides over medium-low heat, warm the half-and-half until steaming hot but not boiling. Reduce the heat to low and add the chocolate, rum, sugar, and coffee. Using an immersion blender, blend the ingredients in the saucepan over very low heat until well blended and frothy. Pour into warm mugs, top with softly whipped cream, and sprinkle a pinch of cayenne over each cup. Serve immediately.

MAKES 4 SERVINGS

Hot Chocolate Reviver

Patty Denny, Telluride Truffles, Telluride, Colorado

Patty Denny's approach to hot chocolate has particular resonance in Telluride, where the famous powder attracts sport adventurists to its 13,000-foot peaks. Since 1997, she has produced decadent chocolate creations from the restaurant kitchen at Telluride Ski Club. Her soul-satisfying hot chocolate, inspired by the mythical barrel of brandy strapped around a Saint Bernard's neck—a symbol of rescue and solace—is enough to revive even the coldest downhill skier on a three-dog night.

Telluride's solemn snow-covered mountains provide the perfect backdrop for blended chocolates spiked with brandy and finished with the distinctively nutty flavor and fragrance of almond oil. Low-fat milk allows more chocolate complexity to shine through, according to Patty, and she advises that the drink is at its best "if swished around in the mouth before swallowing."

3 ounces bittersweet chocolate, coarsely chopped
2 ounces milk chocolate, coarsely chopped
1 cup low-fat organic milk
2 tablespoons brandy
A few drops almond oil

Place both chocolates in a microwave-safe bowl and melt by heating in short bursts, stirring well after each interval. In a saucepan over medium-low heat, warm the milk until it is very hot. Pour the hot milk over the melted chocolate and stir with a wooden spoon until thoroughly combined. Stir in the brandy and almond oil. Pour into a warm mug and serve immediately.

MAKES 1 SERVING

Roasted Hazelnut Hot Chocolate

Dufflet Rosenberg, Dufflet Bakery, Toronto, Canada

Chocolate has many notable affinities, and it blends particularly well with nourishing hazelnuts. Dufflet Rosenberg, owner of Dufflet Bakery, in Toronto, creates a very dark hot chocolate with a subtle woody taste. "Everyone at the bakery agrees it's very sophisticated," she says.

In this recipe, she exploits the sweet, buttery flavor and distinctive, spicy bouquet from roasted hazelnuts, the rich caramel notes from the dark brown sugar, and the complexity of chocolate flavor that results from using both semisweet chocolate pieces and cocoa powder. For a tempting variation, Dufflet suggests omitting the vanilla extract and adding $1/4$ cup of Frangelico, the hazelnut-flavored liqueur, for a hot chocolate that's lost its innocence.

$2^1/2$ ounces whole hazelnuts (about $1/2$ cup)

$4^1/2$ cups whole milk

$1/4$ cup Dutch-process cocoa powder, sifted

$1/4$ cup firmly packed dark brown sugar

$1/4$ cup hot water

4 ounces semisweet chocolate, chopped

1 teaspoon pure vanilla extract

Basic whipped cream for serving (optional) (page 137)

Preheat the oven to 400°F. Spread the hazelnuts on a baking sheet and bake them, stirring occasionally, until the nuts are golden and the skins have cracked, 8 to 10 minutes. Let cool to room temperature. In the bowl of a food processor fitted with the metal blade, process the nuts until finely chopped.

In a heavy saucepan over medium-low heat, stir together the milk and nuts. Bring the mixture to a boil, then remove from the heat and set aside for 30 minutes. Meanwhile, in a small bowl, stir together the cocoa powder and brown sugar. Add the hot water and mix to form a smooth paste. Return the milk mixture to low heat and add the chopped chocolate and the cocoa-sugar paste. Whisk constantly until the chocolate is completely melted and the mixture is very smooth and almost boiling. Remove from the heat and stir in the vanilla. Strain through a fine-mesh sieve directly into large serving cups or mugs. Top with a dollop of whipped cream, if desired, and serve immediately.

MAKES 4 SERVINGS

I drank my morning draft in good chocolate, and, slabbering my band, sent home for another.

SAMUEL PEPYS

Sake-Wasabi Hot Chocolate with Tahini Cookies

Vera Tong, Sushi Samba, New York, Miami, Chicago

The Sushi Samba concept traces its roots to thousands of Japanese who immigrated to South America to cultivate coffee and work on cacao plantations, giving rise to the intermingling of Japanese, Brazilian, and Peruvian cuisines. The dramatic fusion of Asian elegance and South American zest influences the entire Sushi Samba menu, including desserts conceived by pastry chef Vera Tong.

For her hot chocolate, Vera starts with Valrhona Araguani, a grand cru dark chocolate made from Venezuelan cocoa beans. Its powerful bittersweet base, strong licorice, raisin, and chestnut notes, and burnt honey aromas are mellowed by the rich cream of coconut and full-bodied flavor components of cedar-aged Hanahato sake. A lively froth of wasabi-laced milk provides an accent, and tahini cookies are the counterpoint to the creamy drink. NOTE: Wasabi oil is available at Asian markets.

WASABI ESPUMA

1 cup whole milk

2 teaspoons wasabi oil

HOT CHOCOLATE

$7^1/2$ ounces cream of coconut

1 (14-ounce) can coconut milk

1 cinnamon quill

3 ounces Valrhona Araguani chocolate (72 percent cacao)

$1/2$ ounce milk chocolate

$1/2$ cup Hanahato sake

To make the wasabi espuma, combine the milk and wasabi oil in a bowl and whisk until frothy. Pour into a storage container, cover tightly, and refrigerate until ready to use.

To make the hot chocolate, in a saucepan over medium-low heat, combine the cream of coconut, coconut milk, and cinnamon quill and simmer for

CONTINUED

5 to 10 minutes. Turn off the heat and allow to steep for 30 minutes. Reheat the mixture over medium-low heat until it reaches a simmer. Remove from the heat and remove the cinnamon quill. Add the chocolates and blend with an immersion blender until well combined. Add the sake and mix well.

To assemble, release the espuma from its container and spoon on top of the hot chocolate. Serve immediately with the tahini cookies on the side.

MAKES 8 SERVINGS

Tahini Cookies

1³/4 cups all-purpose flour
1 teaspoon baking powder
¹/2 teaspoon baking soda
Pinch of salt
¹/2 cup unsalted butter, room temperature
1 cup firmly packed light brown sugar
¹/4 cup tahini paste
1 large egg
¹/2 cup Japanese roasted black and white sesame seeds

Preheat the oven to 325°F. In a bowl, stir together the flour, baking powder, baking soda, and salt. Set aside. In the bowl of a stand mixer fitted with the paddle attachment, combine the butter, brown sugar, and tahini paste on medium speed until well combined. Add the egg and mix on low speed until fully incorporated. Add the flour mixture and mix until just combined. With your hands, form gumball-size pieces of dough. Roll each ball in the sesame seeds and arrange on a greased baking sheet 2 inches apart. Flatten the balls of dough with the bottom of a glass and bake until golden brown, 7 to 9 minutes.

MAKES 16 COOKIES

Maple-Whiskey Chocolate Hot Toddy

Linda Grishman, Linda Grishman Chocolates, Burlington, Vermont

The best cold weather cure-all, according to chocolatier Linda Grishman, is based upon the simple concept of a hot, sweet alcoholic mixture.

Linda grew up in South Africa, where she remembers a kitchen cabinet always stocked with Cadbury's cocoa, and, despite the country's relatively mild winters, hot chocolate was part of family tradition.

In rural Vermont, calling the doctor is always a last resort, and besides, his remedies are often no better than the maple syrup-and-whiskey cure. Canadian whiskey adds some malt and citrus aromas, while it gives the drink a vaporous warmth and a light smokiness but not too strong a bite. Maple syrup adds notes of honey, sugar, and praline to the blend of dark and milk chocolates.

2 ounces Guittard "Etienne" bittersweet chocolate (61 percent cacao), chopped

2 ounces Guittard "Etienne" milk chocolate (38 percent cacao), chopped

3/4 cup whole milk

1 tablespoon Canadian whiskey

1 tablespoon Grade B maple syrup

Basic whipped cream for serving (page 137)

Fine maple sugar for serving

Place both chocolates in a microwave-safe bowl and melt by heating in short bursts, stirring well after each interval. In a saucepan over medium heat, heat the milk until it is very hot but not boiling. Pour the hot milk over the melted chocolate and stir with a wooden spoon until thoroughly combined. Stir in the whiskey and maple syrup. Pour into a mug, top with a dollop of freshly whipped cream, and sprinkle with maple sugar. Serve immediately.

MAKES 1 SERVING

Hot Chocolate Nightcap Tequila

Maribel Lieberman, MarieBelle, New York, New York

Maribel moved from a small Honduran village to New York City, and she remains connected to her Latin roots even as she operates a sophisticated cacao bar in New York's SoHo neighborhood. Maribel uses Callebaut chocolate as the base for MarieBelle "Aztec" Hot Chocolates, decorative tins of shaved chocolate blends in regular, dark, mocha, and spicy flavors, the last with ancho and chipotle peppers, cinnamon, and nutmeg added. "When you make the drink with water, you really taste the chocolate," she explains. "When you make it with milk, the fat in the milk gently cuts the intense chocolate flavor." A small amount of fine tequila adds exquisite smoky and spicy complexities to the "naughty nightcap," guaranteed to warm up your insides at bedtime.

1/2 cup shaved chocolate, preferably MarieBelle "Aztec" Spicy Hot Chocolate, plus more for coating rims

1 cup whole milk, plus more for coating rims

11/2 ounces tequila

Basic whipped cream for serving (optional; page 137)

In a saucepan over medium-low heat, bring the milk just to a boil. Add the chocolate and stir until thoroughly melted and smooth. Moisten the rims of 2 cups with a bit of milk and dip into additional shaved chocolate to coat. Divide the tequila between the two demitasse cups and divide the hot chocolate between the cups. Top with a dollop of whipped cream, if desired, and serve immediately.

MAKES 2 DEMITASSE SERVINGS

Midnight Cowboy

Ivan and Gus Macias, Tortilla Flats, Santa Fe, New Mexico

"No drink for weaklings," proclaims the menu of Tortilla Flats, where Gus Macias merges Native American and Spanish conquistador cooking and brother Ivan concocts intoxicating hot chocolates for the aid and comfort of all who visit the New Mexican restaurant. Adobe, brick, and ceramic tile in a variety of earth tones set a Southwestern ambience for dining, while three dozen tequilas beckon locals and tourists to the oak bar.

But the Mexican love of drinking chocolates exerts its influence here, and woozy hot chocolate–based "chocktails" take center stage. Consider this drink which has four delicious aromas: the dark molasses notes of Jamaican rum; sweet, creamy Mexican coffee liqueur; the charcoal-mellowed scent of Tennessee sour mash whiskey; and the warm cinnamon perfume of Mexican chocolate.

This drink is about three parts hot chocolate to one part alcohol. Ivan recommends the Midnight Cowboy as an after-dinner drink or with a dessert of flan or hot pie.

1 (3.1-ounce) tablet Mexican chocolate
3/4 cups whole milk
1/2 ounce Meyers dark rum
1/2 ounce Kahlua
1 1/4 ounces Jack Daniel's
Basic whipped cream for serving (page 137)

Break the tablet of Mexican chocolate into small pieces and add it to the milk in a saucepan. Bring the mixture to a simmer over medium-low heat, stirring until the chocolate is melted and the mixture is thoroughly combined. Pour into a mug and stir in the rum, Kahlua, and Jack Daniel's. Top with freshly whipped cream and serve immediately.

MAKES 1 SERVING

Brown Russian

Dan Budd, Taste Budds, Red Hook, New York

In addition to fur hats and thick wool coats, Russians depend on warming spices in their food to help generate inner body heat and comfort throughout the nastiest of winters. The ancient formula for *zbiten*, spiked tea with aromatic spices and nurturing herbs, provided inspiration to Dan Budd, the man at the helm of Taste Budds, an artisan enterprise dedicated to the production of fine chocolates and chocolate desserts.

His contribution to hot chocolate— a restorative with an entirely new personality—is a rich mouthful of chocolate that gets its spellbinding complexity from chai-like spices. For authenticity, serve it in tall Russian coffee glasses.

2 ounces fresh, peeled, sliced ginger

2 cinnamon quills

1/2 teaspoons ground cinnamon

3 whole cloves

1 pinch ground cloves

1/4 teaspoon ground nutmeg

2 bay leaves

3 ounces unsweetened chocolate, finely chopped

6 fresh mint leaves, finely chopped

1/4 cup honey

3 tablespoons sugar

1/8 teaspoon salt

1 cup heavy cream

2 1/2 cups whole milk

1 tablespoon confectioners' sugar

4 tablespoons vodka

Cinnamon for serving

4 small mint sprigs

In a saucepan over medium-low heat, combine the sliced ginger, cinnamon quills, ground cinnamon, whole cloves, ground cloves, nutmeg, and bay leaves. Add 1 cup water and bring to a boil. Immediately turn off the heat, cover, and let steep for 8 minutes.

CONTINUED

Place the chocolate in a medium heatproof bowl and set aside. Add the chopped mint leaves, honey, sugar, salt, 1/2 cup of the cream, and the milk to the saucepan. Return to medium-low heat and stir constantly with a wooden spoon as the mixture comes to a boil. Boil for 10 seconds, then immediately strain the liquid through a fine-mesh sieve onto the chocolate. Whisk slowly until all of the chocolate has melted and is thoroughly incorporated. An immersion blender can be used to smooth the beverage more easily.

In a separate bowl, using an electric mixer, whip the remaining 1/2 cup cream with the confectioners' sugar until it forms very soft peaks. Using a soup spoon, place a generous scoop of whipped cream in the bottom of each of 4 mugs. Add 1 tablespoon vodka on top of the cream. Pour the hot chocolate into the mugs until the whipped cream rises slightly above the rim. Sift a dash of cinnamon on top and garnish with a sprig of mint. Serve immediately.

MAKES 4 SERVINGS

Chestnut Hot Chocolate

Nick Mautone, Trina Restaurant, Fort Lauderdale, Florida

Bon vivant and mixologist Nick Mautone, author of *Raising the Bar*, fondly remembers a store on Second Avenue in Manhattan called Paprika-Weis, which catered to the German and Hungarian immigrants who had settled in the area. In addition to selling paprika from the old country, it also sold other ethnic specialty foods, including chestnut purée in the form of hand-dipped chestnut-stuffed chocolates. According to Nick, "My hot chocolate is the closest you can get to drinking those delicacies out of a mug." Although the drink is exotic and intoxicating on its own, the bartenders at his restaurant Trina will spike it with Frangelico or brandy upon request. NOTE: Chestnut purée is available in many grocery stores. If you have trouble locating it, combine 8 ounces packaged chestnut pieces with 4 ounces water and 1 tablespoon sugar in a food processor fitted with the metal blade, and purée until smooth.

3 cups whole milk
1/2 cup sugar
Pinch of ground cinnamon
Pinch of salt
12 ounces dark chocolate, chopped
12 ounces chestnut purée
4 ounces Frangelico (optional)
4 ounces brandy (optional)
Basic whipped cream for serving (page 137)

In a large saucepan over medium heat, combine the milk, sugar, cinnamon, and salt. Cook, stirring frequently, until the mixture is hot, about 5 minutes. Add the chocolate and cook, stirring constantly, until the chocolate has melted completely. Add the chestnut purée and cook, stirring constantly, until the purée is completely incorporated. Stir in the Frangelico and brandy, if using. Ladle into mugs, top with whipped cream, and serve immediately.

MAKES 8 SERVINGS

Hot Chocolate à l'Orange

Etienne Merle, Restaurateur Emeritus, Ithaca, New York

Eating well is of prime importance in Ithaca, New York, where folks spend an amazing amount of time thinking about, talking about, and consuming food. Natives are still talking about how much they miss L'Auberge du Cochon Rouge, the legendary temple of French cooking and the showcase of an extraordinary chef by the name of Etienne Merle. It was a place where, while Cayuga Lake was freezing over, patrons could feast on stunning French food, then snuggle with a warm intoxicant next to the fireplace to ward off winter, at least for a few precious hours.

Although the restaurant is gone, Etienne continues to dabble in the kitchen of a Cornell fraternity, and he still throws the best dinner parties in town. Cornered in a local market, he agreed to fashion an original hot chocolate recipe for this book, based on, in his words, a "love of hot chocolate and its evolving essays."

Etienne adjusts his orange-flavored renditions of the drink according to the time of day. The daytime version, made with Cointreau, might be generously consumed, for example, from a flask during a Cornell football game. At night, he suggests demitasse servings laced with Grand Marnier. Made this way, the hot chocolate leaves a prolonged aftertaste similar to the effect of tannins in wine.

1/4 cup heavy cream

3/4 cup whole milk

Zest of 1 clementine or Mandarin orange

Pinch of ground cayenne pepper

2 pinches ground nutmeg

Pinch of ground cloves

4 ounces semisweet chocolate (73 percent cacao), chopped

1 ounce Cointreau or Grand Marnier

In a saucepan over medium-low heat, combine the cream, milk, zest, cayenne, nutmeg, and cloves and bring to a simmer. Simmer for 10 minutes, then add the chocolate, stirring continuously with a wooden spoon until thoroughly melted. Stir in the liqueur, pour into a mug, and serve immediately.

MAKES 1 SERVING

Look, there's no metaphysics on earth like chocolates.

FERNANDO PESSOA,
PORTUGUESE POET

Chocolate Irish Coffee

Ghirardelli Chocolate Company, San Francisco, California

A collaboration between two of San Francisco's most revered institutions was inevitable. Ghirardelli Chocolate Company dates back to California's gold rush, when "Domingo" Ghirardelli, an Italian confectioner, began exporting cacao beans and other commodities from South America to supply the needs of the mining communities. He eventually opened a chocolate factory in the city's waterfront district.

Fast forward to 1952, when only a few blocks away Jack Koeppler, owner of the Buena Vista Cafe, and travel writer Stanton Delaplane re-created the "Irish coffee" served at Shannon Airport in Ireland. The mixture of Irish whiskey and strong coffee with heavy cream floating on the surface has been famously served at the Buena Vista ever since.

Recognizing the need for both chocolate *and* coffee at the end of dinner, the folks at Ghirardelli add their Sweet Ground Chocolate and Cocoa to the classic Irish coffee formula, combining complementary flavors into a drink that doubles as dessert.

2 cups freshly brewed coffee

1/4 cup Ghirardelli Sweet Ground Chocolate and Cocoa

2 tablespoons Irish whiskey

1/4 cup basic whipped cream (page 137)

4 teaspoons crème de menthe

Preheat the oven to 250°F and place a small mixing bowl inside to warm, about 5 minutes. In the warmed bowl combine the hot coffee, ground chocolate, and Irish whiskey. Stir until well blended. Pour into tempered glass mugs and top each with 1 tablespoon of the whipped cream. Drizzle the crème de menthe over the whipped cream and serve immediately.

MAKES 2 SERVINGS

Second Childhood

NOSTALGIC HOT CHOCOLATES

Frrrozen Hot Chocolate   87

Mexican Hot Chocolate Fondue   90

Triple Hot Chocolate Obsession   92

Hot Butterscotch with White Chocolate   94

Nutella Hot Chocolate   95

Hot Chocolate Eggnog   96

Key Lime Pie Hot Chocolate   98

Black Bottom Hot Chocolate   100

Skating-on-Thin-Ice Hot Chocolate   103

There's a wonderful alchemy that takes place when hot chocolate is prepared. This ubiquitous comfort food is also extremely versatile. You must respect it, but at the same time, you can have fun with it.

Throughout history, drinking chocolates have appeared in various forms: as a treasure from the gods, an aphrodisiac, a bohemian fancy, a nourishment for children, and, finally, as an appealing elixir that, like Marcel Proust's madeleines, provides a link to a fondly remembered childhood. Here contemporary pastry chefs look at hot chocolate with a child's fresh eye, inventing grown-up versions of the drink that you can enjoy as if tasting liquid chocolate for the first time.

Frrrozen Hot Chocolate

Stephen Bruce, Serendipity 3, New York, New York

Montezuma, emperor of the Aztecs, poured his liquid chocolate over bowls of snow from nearby mountaintops before whipping the mixture into a chilled froth. Five centuries later, a trio of adventurous New York City restaurateurs concocted an icy, wickedly rich confection, keeping its formula a well-guarded secret and thus guaranteeing a faithful following for the legendary dessert.

Stephen Bruce, who founded Serendipity 3 with two partners in 1954, was badgered and begged for his recipe, but for decades he refused to budge—not even for the first lady Jackie Kennedy, who wanted to serve the dessert at a White House function. On the occasion of Serendipity's fiftieth anniversary, however, he finally spilled the beans. Frrrozen Hot Chocolate, it turns out, gets its complex flavor from a dozen different cocoas that are blended with crushed ice to the consistency of a frozen daiquiri. While an authentic reproduction would call for assembling 1/2 ounce each of all twelve cocoas, this version is a little more user-friendly.

Whether sipped through a straw or eaten with a spoon, it's a sweet invitation to childhood.

GANACHE

3 ounces unsweetened cocoa

3 ounces sweetened cocoa

1 1/2 tablespoons sugar

1 tablespoon unsalted butter

1/2 cup whole milk

HOT CHOCOLATE

1 cup whole milk

2 cups crushed ice

Basic whipped cream for serving (page 137)

Chocolate shavings for serving

To make the ganache, in the top of a double boiler over boiling water, combine

CONTINUED

the cocoas, sugar, and butter and melt until it forms a smooth paste. Slowly drizzle the milk into the chocolate mixture, stirring constantly until thoroughly blended and smooth as silk. Cool to room temperature.

To make the drink, combine $1/2$ cup of the ganache with the milk and crushed ice in a blender and blend on high speed until the mixture is the consistency of a frozen daiquiri. Pour into a large goblet, top with a mound of whipped cream, and sprinkle with chocolate shavings. Serve with 2 straws for sipping and an iced-tea spoon for devouring.

MAKES 1 LARGE SERVING

For invalids and persons of delicate digestion, breakfast cocoa is very nourishing and easily assimilated. Owing to its concentrated nutriment, it becomes, when milk is added, an almost perfect food.

HERSHEY'S BREAKFAST COCOA ADVERTISEMENT, 1926

Mexican Hot Chocolate Fondue

Gale Gand, Tru, Chicago, Illinois

Ice skating in Jewett Park until her toes were numb, then warming up with a cup of hot chocolate in the field house—that's one of Gale Gand's vivid memories of growing up in Chicago.

An update of retro dessert fondues, her explosively flavorful, Mexican-inspired liquid chocolate provides dinner parties with dessert-as-entertainment. "Many things happen at the table that can't happen anywhere else," says Gale, who recommends serving the fondue on a round table, where all guests have an equal access to the pot with their fondue dippers.

CHOCOLATE FONDUE

1/3 cup sugar

1 tablespoon cornstarch

1 1/4 cups heavy cream

1 1/4 cups whole milk

2 tablespoons freshly brewed coffee

1/2 teaspoon ground Ceylon cinnamon or canela

1 vanilla bean, split lengthwise

7 ounces bittersweet chocolate, chopped

3 tablespoons unsalted butter

DIPPERS

Banana slices

Manzano or red banana slices

Strawberries with stem

Marshmallows

Toasted cubes of pound cake

Pineapple chunks

Anjou or Bartlett pear slices

Fried wonton wrappers

Bing cherries with stem

In a bowl, whisk together the sugar and cornstarch to blend. Slowly whisk in the cream, then the milk, coffee, cinnamon, and vanilla bean. Pour the mixture into a stainless-steel saucepan and gently bring to a boil over medium-low heat. Cook, whisking constantly until thickened, about 4 minutes. Remove the pan from the heat and whisk in the chocolate and butter until melted. Pour through a fine-mesh sieve into a large bowl and discard the solids. Pour into a warmed fondue pot and serve immediately with assorted foods for dipping and fondue forks.

MAKES 2 SERVINGS

He turned round, and leaning upon his elbow, began to sip his chocolate. The mellow November sun came streaming into the room. The sky was bright, and there was a genial warmth in the air. It was almost like a morning in May.

OSCAR WILDE, *THE PICTURE OF DORIAN GRAY*

Triple Hot Chocolate Obsession

Joanne Chang, Flour Bakery, Boston, Massachusetts

Any mention of hot chocolate and Joanne Chang, owner of Flour Bakery in Boston's South End, will admit she grew up, like many of us, on Swiss Miss. "Then, when I first got into pastry, I remember learning how to make ganache as the basis of hot chocolate. I was blown away by the intensity and richness of the real thing."

Joanne's layered hot chocolate is based on a familiar triple chocolate cake done up "Flour style," with an outburst of individuality. It makes eloquent use of three distinct chocolate flavors in playful harmony. She explains, "I want you to try one taste, compare it to the other, compare that to the third, and then remain undecided about which is the most delicious and try the whole tasting all over again."

WHITE CHOCOLATE WHIPPED CREAM

3 ounces white chocolate, chopped

1 teaspoon pure vanilla extract

1 cup heavy cream

GANACHE

4 ounces bittersweet chocolate, chopped

1/2 cup heavy cream

MILK CHOCOLATE HOT CHOCOLATE

4 ounces milk chocolate, chopped

4 cups whole milk

Shaved white chocolate for serving

Shaved milk chocolate for serving

Shaved dark chocolate for serving

To make the white chocolate whipped cream, place the white chocolate and vanilla in a small heatproof bowl. In a small saucepan over medium-low heat, bring the cream to just under the boiling point. Pour the hot cream over the white chocolate and whisk until thoroughly combined. Refrigerate overnight.

To make the ganache, place the chocolate in a small heatproof bowl. In a small saucepan over medium-low heat, bring the cream to just under the boiling point. Pour the hot cream over the chocolate and whisk until thoroughly combined. Set aside.

To make the milk chocolate hot chocolate, place the milk chocolate in a small heatproof bowl. In a small saucepan over medium-low heat, bring the milk to just under the boiling point. Pour the hot milk over the milk chocolate and whisk until thoroughly combined.

To make the triple chocolate hot chocolate, divide the ganache evenly among 4 mugs. Heat the milk chocolate hot chocolate to just under the boiling point and divide among the mugs. Remove the white chocolate whipped cream from the refrigerator and whip with an electric mixer until it is thick and holds a peak. Divide among the mugs. Sprinkle white, milk, and dark chocolate shavings on top of each mug and serve immediately.

MAKES 4 SERVINGS

Hot Butterscotch with White Chocolate

Julie Hasson, cookbook author, Los Angeles, California

"Chocolate makes people feel happy," says Julie Hasson, who grew up in Southern California, where she and her family used to pretend it was winter so they could make hot chocolate.

In this recipe, Julie captures memories of a youthful love of butterscotch in a high-pitched adult hot chocolate that hits all the right notes. In it, she uses white chocolate to good advantage, and she transforms brusque Scotch into its willing, lyrical partner. "Some people think white chocolate is mild, but it actually has a vibrant, assertive taste," insists Julie.

1 cup whole milk

1/2 cup heavy cream

1/4 cup firmly packed brown sugar

1 ounce white chocolate, chopped

1 tablespoon Scotch whiskey

Basic whipped cream for serving (optional; page 137)

In a small saucepan, whisk together the milk, cream, and brown sugar. Place the saucepan over medium heat and bring to a simmer. Reduce the heat to low, add the white chocolate, and whisk until the chocolate is melted and the mixture is smooth and steaming hot. Remove the saucepan from the heat. Whisk in the Scotch whiskey and pour into mugs. Top with whipped cream, if desired, and serve immediately.

MAKES 2 SERVINGS

Nutella Hot Chocolate

Chuck Silverston, Paris Crêperie, Brookline, Massachusetts

During World War II, cocoa was in short supply, and chocolate was limited by rationing. To create an economical alternative, Italian pastry maker Pietro Ferrero blended cocoa with more readily available hazelnuts, cocoa butter, and vegetable oils. Ferrero's "Supercrema Gianduja"—renamed Nutella in 1964—became so popular that children would line up at the local grocery with a piece of bread for a smear of the tasty paste. The chocolate-hazelnut spread has since become a breakfast favorite in Germany and a popular after-school snack in both Italy and France. Worldwide, it outsells all peanut butter brands combined.

Brookline's Paris Crêperie melts Nutella into soothing cups of warm milk, then uses the cappuccino steamer to raise a bubbly froth. "The nutty perfume is heavenly in hot chocolate," says owner Chuck Silverston, who invented the minimalist delight. "I can't believe someone didn't think of this before." During the summer, the restaurant offers a Nutella Frozen Hot Chocolate, made the same way but with the addition of vanilla ice cream and plain yogurt.

3/4 cup whole milk
2 heaping tablespoons Nutella
Basic whipped cream for serving (page 137)

In a small saucepan over medium-low heat, bring the milk to a simmer. Add the Nutella and stir with a wooden spoon until thoroughly blended. Pour into a mug and garnish with a dollop of whipped cream. Serve immediately.

MAKES 1 SERVING

Hot Chocolate Eggnog

Lee Posey, Pearl Bakery, Portland, Oregon

It's a drink with a pedigree: Eggnog was brought from England to America, where it became a favorite wintertime drink of the colonists. George Washington is known to have devised his own recipe for eggnog that included rye whiskey, rum, and sherry. An English visitor to the United States reported in 1866, "Christmas is not properly observed unless you brew egg nogg for all comers."

In this recipe, Lee Posey marries hot chocolate to ancestral eggnog in a rich, soulful interpretation that's heightened with a magical pinch of nutmeg. She insists on freshly grating whole nutmeg for its warm, pleasantly bitter flavor and musky aroma. If you have never experienced freshly grated nutmeg, you will be amazed at its spicy-sweet intensity. It smells like the Christmases of childhood.

2 cups whole milk

1/2 cup heavy cream

1/4 cup sugar

1/4 teaspoon freshly grated nutmeg

1/2 vanilla bean

6 large egg yolks

3 ounces bittersweet chocolate (60 percent cacao), chopped

Unsweetened whipped cream for serving

Freshly grated nutmeg for serving

In a small saucepan, combine the milk, cream, sugar, and nutmeg. Split the vanilla bean lengthwise and scrape the seeds into the milk mixture. Add the vanilla pod to the milk mixture and bring to a simmer over medium-low heat. Remove from the heat and set aside to steep for about 20 minutes. Return to a simmer over medium heat. After the mixture is hot, remove a small amount, whisk into egg yolks, then return the egg yolk mixture to the milk mixture. Cook, stirring constantly, until slightly thickened, about 5 minutes. Remove from the heat, add the chocolate, and let sit for a few seconds, until the chocolate melts. Whisk to combine, then pour into mugs through a fine-mesh sieve. Top with whipped cream and freshly grated nutmeg and serve immediately.

MAKES 4 SERVINGS

Animal crackers, and cocoa to drink
That is the finest of suppers, I think
When I'm grown up and can have
  what I please,
I think I shall always insist upon these.

CHRISTOPHER MORLEY

Key Lime Pie Hot Chocolate

Hedy Goldsmith, NEMO, Prime 112, Shoji Sushi, Miami Beach, Florida

At three sister restaurants in Miami, pastry chef Hedy Goldsmith, whose desserts have been hailed by the *New York Times* as "strikingly beautiful but not contrived… marvels of texture and balance," finds her influences in Miami's geographical bearing and tropical vibe. Her riffs on native Key lime have included everything from Key Lime Crème Brûlée to Key Lime Tiramisu.

Her hot chocolate recipe has all the ingredients and sweet goodness of a classic Key Lime Pie: graham crackers, sweetened condensed milk, and Key lime juice. "Together, the chocolate and citrus are sensual and intriguing," says Hedy, "while still remaining comfortable and familiar."

Zest of 10 Key limes
1 cup whole milk
1 vanilla bean, split lengthwise
Pinch of salt
1/4 cup sugar
1/4 cup unsweetened cocoa powder
31/2 ounces bittersweet chocolate (70 percent cacao), chopped
1/2 cup sweetened condensed milk, or to taste
3 tablespoons freshly squeezed Key lime juice, plus more for coating rims
Graham cracker crumbs

In a medium saucepan over medium-low heat, combine 1 cup water with the lime zest and bring to a boil. Cover, remove from the heat, and let steep for 15 minutes. Return to heat and add the milk, vanilla bean, salt, and sugar. Return to boil. Add the cocoa powder and chocolate, whisking to combine as the mixture returns to a boil. Remove from heat. Remove the vanilla bean and discard.

Place the mixture in a blender and blend for 5 minutes at medium speed. Add the sweetened condensed milk and the Key lime juice and blend for another 1 minute. Take 4 demitasse cups and rim each one with Key lime juice. Dip the rims into the crushed graham cracker crumbs. Fill with the foamy hot chocolate and serve immediately.

MAKES 4 DEMITASSE SERVINGS

Foamy, creamy-rich cocoa is a wonderful food with which to woo finicky child-appetites—an easy and delicious way of helping to include the daily quart of milk in their meals.

WALTER BAKER & CO. PROMOTIONAL BOOKLET, 1931

Black Bottom Hot Chocolate

Mindy Segal, HOTCHOCOLATE, Chicago, Illinois

"I have major respect for technique, and respect for culinary history," says Mindy Segal, who in 2005 launched a neighborhood gathering spot called HOTCHOCOLATE, an eclectic dessert-centered restaurant in Chicago's Bucktown. There, in a playful, edgy atmosphere, she breathes new life into classics and presents familiar flavors with an intellectual twist.

A pleasure-packed testament to her nimbleness of imagination and execution is this fusion of two familiar treats. Hot fudge and hot chocolate become partners in a voluptuous two-toned dessert. "The double dose of chocolate, the play on temperatures and textures, and the fun twist it gives to a classic hot chocolate," observes Mindy, "all reflect my passion and my style."

FUDGE

3 cups heavy cream

1 1/2 cups sugar

1/4 cup light corn syrup

5 ounces unsweetened chocolate, chopped

1 to 3 teaspoons salt

2 tablespoons pure vanilla extract

1/2 cup unsalted butter

HOT CHOCOLATE

1 1/2 cups whole milk

1/2 cup heavy cream

2 tablespoons firmly packed light brown sugar

2 ounces bittersweet chocolate (62 percent cacao), chopped

6 ounces milk chocolate, chopped

Basic whipped cream for serving (page 137)

To make the fudge, in a heavy saucepan over medium-low heat, heat the cream and sugar, stirring to dissolve. Add corn syrup and stir to dissolve. Add chocolate and stir to combine. Bring the mixture to a boil. Once it reaches a boil, lower the heat to a simmer. It is important to stir frequently to avoid scalding. When the mixture begins to separate, add the vanilla and butter and stir to thoroughly combine. Add salt to taste; it should be slightly salty. Pour one-quarter of the fudge into each demitasse cup and refrigerate until set, about 1 hour.

To make the hot chocolate, in a saucepan over medium-low heat, bring the milk, cream, and brown sugar to a boil. Add the chocolates, turn off the heat, and let chocolate steep in the liquid for about 1 minute. Using an immersion blender, whisk to combine.

To serve, pour the hot chocolate into the fudge-layered cups. Top with a dollop of whipped cream and serve immediately with a spoon.

MAKES 4 DEMITASSE SERVINGS

Cocoa? Cocoa! Damn miserable puny stuff, fit for kittens and unwashed boys. Did Shakespeare drink cocoa?

SHIRLEY JACKSON

Skating-on-Thin-Ice Hot Chocolate

Elizabeth Falkner, Citizen Cake, San Francisco, California

In San Francisco, the appetite for fine food is every bit as robust as the craving for fine art, if not more so. Avant-garde pastry chef Elizabeth Falkner aims to satisfy both desires at her dessert restaurant called Citizen Cake, where she transforms the visions in her head into culinary fireworks. "I like to consider pushing the envelope of how we perceive the sweet stuff," she explains, "and offer alternative representations to what is usually expected only on the plate."

Everything about this passionate artist is ferociously inventive, including the way she names recipes. Her witty, hot-and-cold showpiece she calls Skating-on-Thin-Ice Hot Chocolate borrows from the composition of a parfait for its construction. Each bite is a wild ride for the taste buds, an outburst of bitter, malted flavors mellowed by the vanilla-scented ice milk and the smooth liquid chocolate.

ICE MILK

1/2 cup heavy cream

2 teaspoons sugar

1/2 teaspoon pure vanilla extract

1 tablespoon sour cream

1 cup whole or low-fat milk

CAROB GANACHE

1/2 cup heavy cream

1 ounce bittersweet chocolate, chopped

1 ounce milk chocolate

2 ounces carob chips

Pinch of kosher salt

HOT CHOCOLATE

1 tablespoon malt powder or carob powder

2 teaspoons firmly packed brown sugar

1 tablespoon unsweetened cocoa powder

1 ounce bittersweet chocolate, chopped

Pinch of kosher salt

1/2 cup whole or low-fat milk

CONTINUED

4 malt balls

1/2 cup chocolate-covered raisins

To make the ice milk, combine the cream and sugar in a saucepan over medium-low heat and bring to a boil, stirring to dissolve. Add the vanilla, sour cream, and milk and stir together. Pour into a shallow dish or ice cube tray and freeze.

To make the carob ganache, in a saucepan over medium-low heat, bring the cream to a boil. Pour over the chopped chocolates and carob in a heatproof bowl to melt. Add the salt and stir until smooth.

To make the hot chocolate, in a saucepan over medium-low heat, combine 1/3 cup water with the malt powder, brown sugar, and cocoa powder and bring to a boil while whisking. Turn off heat and add the chocolate, stirring to dissolve. Add the salt and milk just before serving and bring to a boil.

To assemble, break the ice milk into chunks and put a few pieces in four 4-ounce glasses, cups, or cordial glasses. Place a malt ball and a few chocolate-covered raisins in each glass with the ice milk. Pipe some of the carob ganache over the surface of the ice milk. Pour the hot chocolate gently into each glass and serve immediately with a demitasse spoon on the side.

MAKES 4 SERVINGS

Convivial Companions

HOT CHOCOLATE PAIRINGS

▬ ▬ ▬ ▬ ▬ ▬ ▬ ▬ ▬ ▬

Hot Chocolate Dulce de Leche with Cherry-Chocolate Ricotta Beignet   107

Iced Chocolate with Nibby Cookies   110

Fatale Chocolate with Catalan Cloud   112

Mariposa Hot Chocolate with Hot! Chocolate Cookies   114

"New" Mexican Hot Chocolate with Cinnamon-Dusted Churros   117

Hot Chocolate with Tuile Cookies   120

Grand Finale Hot Chocolate with Marshmallow Cream   122

S'Mores Hot Chocolate with Graham Crackers   125

Warm Bittersweet Chocolate Custard with Toasted Chile Pepper Marshmallows and Cheese Arepa   127

Reception Hot Chocolate with Coconut Marshmallow   130

Maple Milk Chocolate Pudding/Dipping Sauce with Crispy Bacon Lardons   134

WHIPPED CREAM MENU   137

Basic	Cayenne
Chocolate	Bourbon
Cinnamon	Ginger

Proper drinking chocolate is so rich and vigorous that it needs a little something assertive as a counterpoint. Make the right choice and you add both visual and gustatory pizzazz to the hot chocolate ritual.

Sipping hot chocolate through cool, lightly whipped cream is a remarkable sensation, while bobbing for marshmallows in the lush liquid provides a playful encounter. Experience an aspect of Spanish culture by dunking *churros* into hot chocolate for breakfast, or unwind with the American marriage of hot chocolate and cookies at bedtime. Whether traditional or unfamiliar, the following thoughtful pairings result in a nurturing, soothing, and satisfying experience.

Hot Chocolate Dulce de Leche with Cherry-Chocolate Ricotta Beignet

Karen Krasne, Extraordinary Desserts, San Diego, California

Karen Krasne finds creative inspiration in the melding of a background in classic French pastry and experience in the tropics of Hawaii and Mexico. She stretches the definition of hot chocolate with this indulgent blend of Valrhona dark chocolate, Mexican cajeta (caramelized milk), a hint of cinnamon, and a splash of rum. The Cherry-Chocolate Ricotta Beignet complements the flavors of the hot chocolate, and the combination of the two is neither too sweet nor too intense.

HOT CHOCOLATE

1 tablespoon sugar

2 tablespoons, plus 2 cups heavy cream

1 cup Valrhona chocolate (70 percent cacao), chopped

1 teaspoon Myers rum

1 teaspoon pure vanilla extract

1 teaspoon ground cinnamon

1 tablespoon cajeta (dulce de leche)

Whipped cream for serving

Place sugar in a saucepan over high heat and, watching closely, allow sugar to caramelize for 7 to 10 minutes, until golden brown. Remove from heat. Add 2 tablespoons of the cream to the caramelized sugar and stir until incorporated. Add the chocolate, stirring constantly until completely melted. Return the mixture to the heat and stir in the remaining 2 cups cream, the rum, and vanilla. Continue to stir until the mixture begins to thicken, about 5 to 7 minutes. Remove the mixture from the heat and stir in the cinnamon and cajeta. If the liquid is too thick, stir in a small amount of water until the desired consistency is reached. Pour into demitasse cups, top with whipped cream, and serve immediately with the beignets.

MAKES 4 TO 6 DEMITASSE SERVINGS

CONTINUED

Hot Chocolate Dulce de Leche with Cherry-Chocolate Ricotta Beignet, *continued*

Cherry-Chocolate Ricotta Beignet

2 cups ricotta cheese
4 1/2 tablespoons all-purpose flour
6 1/2 tablespoons granulated sugar
3/4 cup sun-dried cherries
3/4 cup semisweet chocolate chips
1 tablespoon cherry liqueur
1 (17.5-ounce) package of puff pastry, thawed
Vegetable or canola oil for deep-frying
Confectioners' sugar for dusting

In a bowl, stir together the ricotta, flour, sugar, cherries, chocolate chips, and cherry liqueur until well combined. Set aside.

Cut puff pastry into 8 4-inch squares. Place 2 tablespoons of the ricotta mixture on each puff pastry square, fold in half, and pinch together the edges to seal. Arrange the beignets in a single layer on a baking sheet, cover, and allow to set in the refrigerator for 1 hour. Heat 2 inches of the oil in a saucepan until oil reaches 400°F on a deep-frying thermometer. Remove the beignets from the refrigerator and, using tongs, submerge them in the oil for 5 minutes, or until dough turns golden brown. Drain them on paper towels and dust with confectioners' sugar. Serve immediately.

MAKES 8 BEIGNETS

Iced Chocolate with Nibby Cookies

Arnon Oren, Café Cacao, Berkeley, California

Café Cacao is housed at one end of the Scharffen Berger chocolate factory, so customers are greeted by the seductive aromas of roasting beans. Once inside, you can order an all-chocolate meal of a grilled nectarine salad with arugula, house-cured pancetta, and cocoa nibs, followed by chocolate pasta with sweet-and-sour beef ragout. Save room, of course, for a chocolate dessert.

Iced chocolate at Café Cacao is an echo of the cold comfort of *choco*, the summertime drink of Arnon Oren's youth in Rosh Pina, a small town in northern Israel.

Roasted cacao beans separated from their husks and broken into small bits are called "nibs." They add crunchiness and subtle chocolate flavor to Arnon's salad and make a great substitute for chocolate chips, without the added sweetness. At Café Cacao, the chef's Iced Chocolate and Nibby Cookies were made for each other.

ICED CHOCOLATE

6 cups whole milk

1/4 cup granulated sugar

1 cup Scharffen Berger unsweetened cocoa powder

Ice for serving

In a saucepan, warm 2 cups of the milk over medium-low heat. Add the sugar to the milk and stir to dissolve. Add the cocoa powder and stir to make a paste. Remove from heat and stir in the remaining 4 cups of chilled milk. Pour the liquid over ice and serve immediately.

VARIATION: To make an iced chocolate mocha, simply replace 1/2 cup milk with your favorite brewed coffee. Let the mixture cool before pouring over the ice cubes. Garnish with whipped cream and grated chocolate.

MAKES 4 SERVINGS

Nibby Cookies

1 cup firmly packed dark brown sugar

3/4 cup granulated sugar

1 cup cold unsalted butter, cut into
tablespoon-size chunks

1 tablespoon pure vanilla extract

2 large eggs

3 cups all-purpose flour

1/4 teaspoon salt

3/4 teaspoon baking soda

1/2 cup Scharffen Berger Cacao Nibs

Preheat the oven to 350°F. Measure both sugars into the bowl of a food processor fitted with a metal blade and start processing. Drop the butter into the feeding tube, 1 chunk at a time, until the butter and sugar are blended. Stop the processor while you add the eggs and the vanilla into the feeding tube. Process for 15 seconds, scrape down the sides of the bowl, and process for 10 seconds more. Remove the cover and add the flour to the bowl of the processor. Add the salt and baking soda to the flour, briefly mixing them together with your measuring spoon. Cover and process for 30 seconds. Scrape down the sides and process for 10 seconds more. Open the cover, add the nibs, and process for 15 seconds. Drop tablespoon-size portions of dough onto greased baking sheets. Bake the cookies until fully set, 8 to 12 minutes. Allow to cool on the baking sheet for 5 minutes before transferring to a wire rack to cool completely.

MAKES 4 DOZEN COOKIES

Fatale Chocolate with Catalan Cloud

Michelle Myers, Sona Restaurant, Los Angeles, California

Michelle Myers's fine-arts background—she is trained as a classical pianist and an art preservationist—shows up in her proficiently crafted hot chocolate.

A fascinating stylist, Michelle adapts "crème brûlée" flavors from the Catalan region of Spain to create a poetic foam that gets spooned over the top of a hot chocolate infused with *fatale*, a habañero-like pepper from Chino Ranch Farmer's Market in Rancho Santa Fe. The flavors come in two waves: a cool blast from the froth followed by a hot rush from the chocolate.

NOTE: Lecithin, available in the international section of most grocery stores, allows foam to retain its volume. Be careful not to add too much because it can affect the flavor.

HOT CHOCOLATE

2 cups whole milk

1/4 cup heavy cream

1/2 cup sugar

1 vanilla bean, halved lengthwise

1 fatale, Scotch bonnet, or habañero chile

4 ounces El Rey bittersweet chocolate (70 percent cacao)

CATALAN CLOUD

2 cups whole milk

1 cinnamon quill

A few slices of fresh ginger

2 teaspoons grated orange zest

2 teaspoons grated lemon zest

1/4 vanilla bean, halved lengthwise

1 teaspoon soy lecithin

To make the hot chocolate, in a heavy saucepan over medium-low heat, combine the milk, cream, sugar, and vanilla bean and bring to a simmer, stirring occasionally. Add the whole pepper, allow to steep for a few seconds, then remove both the pepper and the vanilla bean. Strain mixture to remove seeds. Add chocolate and stir constantly until it is completely melted and the mixture is smooth. Keep warm over very low heat.

To make the Catalan cloud, in a saucepan over medium heat, combine the milk, cinnamon quill, ginger, orange and lemon zests, vanilla bean, and soy lecithin. Simmer for 8 to 10 minutes, then strain into a bowl through a fine-mesh sieve. Use an emulsion blender to blend the liquid until frothy.

To serve, pour the hot chocolate into demitasse cups, spoon the Catalan cloud on top, and serve immediately.

MAKES 4 DEMITASSE SERVINGS

Hot chocolate means more than something good to drink. It means energy—a healthful stimulus to appetites—soothing nourishment at night to tired nerves.

FROM "FAMOUS CHOCOLATE RECIPES," GENERAL FOODS, 1936

Mariposa Hot Chocolate with Hot! Chocolate Cookies

Letty Halloran Flatt, Deer Valley Resort, Park City, Utah

Letty Flatt's kitchen is responsible for Deer Valley slope-side service of old-fashioned hot cocoas that warm hands and spirits during the day, as well as seeing to après-ski fireside hot cocoas in the cheerful confines of the lodge.

For Deer Valley's Mariposa restaurant, Letty concocts an even more powerful expression of simmering chocolate and cream, served in a 4-ounce espresso cup alongside a snowflake-shaped shortbread cookie with a slight hint of heat from cayenne pepper. Like skiing in deep, fluffy powder, enjoying this combo is a great rush.

HOT CHOCOLATE

1/2 cup heavy cream

6 ounces bittersweet chocolate, chopped

13/4 cups whole milk

1 tablespoon unsweetened cocoa powder

1 teaspoon pure vanilla extract

2 tablespoons coffee-flavored liqueur

In a large saucepan over medium-low heat, heat the cream until it is very hot, but do not allow it to come to a boil. Remove from the heat. Whisk about one-fourth of the chocolate into the cream until it melts. Add the remaining chocolate and whisk until all of the chocolate has melted and the ganache is smooth and glossy. In a clean saucepan over medium heat, whisk the milk and cocoa powder together and heat until the milk is almost boiling. Pour over the ganache and stir in the vanilla and liqueur. Return the saucepan to medium heat and whisk gently until the hot chocolate is smooth and hot. Pour into mugs and serve immediately with a cookie on the side. If not serving immediately, keep hot in a double boiler until ready to serve, up to several hours.

MAKES 6 DEMITASSE SERVINGS

Hot! Chocolate Cookies

1 cup unsalted butter, at room temperature

1/2 cup granulated sugar

1/3 cup firmly packed brown sugar

1 large egg

1 teaspoon pure vanilla extract

2 cups all-purpose flour

3 tablespoons unsweetened cocoa powder

1 teaspoon ground cinnamon

3/4 teaspoon salt

3/8 teaspoon ground cayenne pepper

1/4 teaspoon freshly ground black pepper

4 ounces bittersweet chocolate, grated

Canola oil for greasing (optional)

In a large bowl, using an electric mixer, cream the butter and sugars until light and fluffy. Beat in the egg and vanilla, scraping the sides and bottom of the bowl as needed. In a separate bowl, sift together the flour, cocoa powder, cinnamon, salt, cayenne, and black peppers. Stir the dry ingredients into the creamed butter mixture until the dough comes together, scraping the side of the bowl as needed. Stir in the grated chocolate. Wrap the dough in plastic wrap and refrigerate until the dough is very cold, at least 3 hours.

Preheat the oven to 325°F. Line 2 large baking sheets with parchment paper or grease them lightly with canola oil. Divide the dough into 4 portions and shape each into a round disk. Return 3 portions to the refrigerator while you work the fourth. On a lightly floured surface, roll the dough to about 1/8 inch thick. With a snowflake-shaped cutter, cut out cookies. Transfer the snowflakes to the baking sheets, arranging them about 1/2 inch apart. Gather the scraps and refrigerate.

CONTINUED

Bake the cookies until they have lost their wet shine and you can slide a cookie on the baking sheet without it losing its shape, 12 to 15 minutes. Roll, cut, and bake the other portions of dough as you did the first. Reroll, cut, and bake the scraps when they are cold again. If you prefer not to roll out the dough, you can divide it into 2 portions and form each into a log 1 1/4 inches in diameter. Refrigerate the logs until they are firm enough to slice, slice into rounds 1/2 inch thick, and bake as directed. Cool for 3 minutes on baking sheets, then transfer to wire racks.

MAKES 6 DOZEN COOKIES.

Say what you will it is pleasant to awake every morning, to take early breakfast in the balcony room with the sweet fresh air coming up from the garden through the open glass door; to drink, instead of coffee, a cup of chocolate handed one on a tray.

TONY IN THOMAS MANN'S *BUDDENBROOKS*

"New" Mexican Hot Chocolate with Cinnamon-Dusted Churros

David Guas, Ceiba, Washington, D.C.

As an executive pastry chef, David Guas combines flavors from Brazil, Peru, Cuba, and the Yucatan. Combining his Cuban heritage with the culinary skills he picked up cooking in New Orleans, New York, Indonesia, and France, David demonstrates the value of moderation. He commits no extravagance with his partnership of contemporary Mexican-inspired drinking chocolate and authentic Mexican fried crullers called *churros*.

For the hot chocolate recipe, he uses just enough heavy cream to thicken the brew, providing an ideal coating for his warm *churros*. Aromatic vanilla and cinnamon and the nuttiness imparted by a few drops of almond extract allow the seductive character of Venezuelan chocolate to arouse the senses. Tradition is exalted, as a 4-ounce portion of the liquid is served in clear demitasse cups with *churros* on the side for dunking.

HOT CHOCOLATE

2/3 cup whole milk

1 cup heavy cream

Pinch of shredded canela

1/8 vanilla bean, halved lengthwise

4 ounces semisweet chocolate, chopped

1/3 teaspoon almond extract

Basic whipped cream for serving (page 137)

Ground cinnamon for serving

In a stainless-steel saucepan over medium-low heat, combine the milk, cream, canela, and vanilla bean and bring to a boil. Remove from the heat and allow the mixture to steep for 5 minutes. Meanwhile, place the chocolate in a heat-proof bowl. When the liquid has finished steeping, pour it over the chocolate and stir until the chocolate is completely melted and smooth. Add the almond extract.

CONTINUED

Strain through a fine-mesh sieve. The hot chocolate is ready to be served now, or it can be refrigerated, covered, until ready to serve. To reheat, warm in a saucepan over low heat, stirring constantly so that it doesn't burn. Pour the hot chocolate into demitasse cups and top with a dollop of slightly sweetened, softly whipped cream and a light dusting of cinnamon. Serve immediately with warm churros.

MAKES 4 DEMITASSE SERVINGS

Cinnamon-Dusted Churros

2 cups water

1 1/2 teaspoons salt

2 cups all-purpose flour

1 tablespoon ground cinnamon

1 cup sugar

Canola oil or other neutral oil for deep-frying

In a saucepan over high heat, bring the water and salt to a boil, and hold at a boil for 4 minutes. Gradually add the flour, stirring vigorously with a wooden spoon until a ball forms. Once the flour is fully incorporated, turn it out onto a cutting board. Allow to cool slightly, then knead by hand for 3 to 4 minutes. Put the dough into a pastry bag fitted with a 3/8-inch star tip. In a shallow bowl, stir together the cinnamon and sugar.

Pour the oil into a skillet to a depth of at least 2 inches and heat until it measures 400°F on a deep-frying thermometer. Pipe the dough directly into the oil, using a knife to cut the dough into 4-inch lengths. Fry the churros 3 or 4 at a time, turning so that they cook evenly, until they are golden brown, 2 to 3 minutes. Remove from oil, drain on paper towels for 30 seconds, toss in the cinnamon-sugar mixture, and serve warm with hot chocolate for dunking.

MAKES 8 TO 10 CHURROS

Hot Chocolate with Tuile Cookies

Tim Partridge, Perdix, Boston, Massachusetts

Tim Partridge, chef/owner of Perdix, recalls growing up in Swansea, Massachusetts, when Fridays were set aside for family night. Everyone would gather in front of the fireplace to play board games, while his mom served fresh-baked Italian bread with homemade jam and steaming hot chocolate. At Perdix (the name means *partridge* in Latin), he serves that fondly remembered hot chocolate, adapted for grown-up tastes. "You ought to have some connection to the food you prepare," says Tim.

This intense drink, the chocolate equivalent of an espresso, is served with thin, crispy chocolate-chip cookies on the side. He claims that having hot chocolate with cookies on the menu lets his customers know that the restaurant is not taking itself too seriously: "It tells them that we're willing to have some fun with what we're doing."

HOT CHOCOLATE

1 1/2 cups whole milk

1/2 cup heavy cream

8 teaspoons granulated sugar

1 tablespoon firmly packed brown sugar

2 tablespoons semisweet chocolate chips

2 tablespoons unsweetened chocolate chips

1/2 teaspoon pure vanilla extract

Marshmallows for serving (optional)

Ground cinnamon for serving (optional)

Unsweetened cocoa powder for serving (optional)

In a heavy saucepan over medium-low heat, combine the milk, cream, sugars, and chocolates and bring to a simmer. Remove the mixture from the heat. Pour half of the mixture into a blender and blend until frothy. Pour the frothed mixture into the saucepan with the rest of the liquid. Add the vanilla and stir to combine. Pour into demitasse cups and garnish with marshmallows and a sprinkling of cinnamon and cocoa powder, if desired. Serve immediately with tuile cookies.

MAKES 4 DEMITASSE SERVINGS

Tuile Cookies

$1/2$ cup unsalted butter, at room temperature, plus more for greasing

$1/2$ cup granulated sugar

$1/2$ cup firmly packed brown sugar

1 large egg

1 teaspoon pure vanilla extract

$3/4$ cup all-purpose flour

$1/2$ teaspoon baking soda

1 cup semisweet chocolate chips

Preheat the oven to 375°F. Butter a baking sheet and line with parchment paper. In a large bowl, combine the butter and the sugars. With a handheld electric mixer on high speed, beat until smooth. Add the egg and the vanilla and beat until well blended. In a separate small bowl, combine the flour and baking soda. Add the flour mixture to the butter mixture and beat on medium speed until thoroughly combined. Add the chocolate chips and beat until fully incorporated. Drop tablespoons of batter onto the prepared cookie sheet and bake until the tuiles are golden and crisp, 12 minutes. Cool on a baking sheet for 3 minutes, then transfer to wire rack.

MAKES 12 COOKIES

Grand Finale Hot Chocolate with Marshmallow Cream

Nicole Coady, Finale Desserterie, Cambridge, Massachusetts

Nicole Coady has been smitten with hot chocolate ever since her childhood in West Virginia, where she remembers her grandmother at the stove, melting chocolate bars into milk. She recalls huddling on the living room floor with her two sisters and her brother, their hands wrapped around mugs of the warming liquid.

Her evocative hot drink starts with Valrhona Equatoriale Chocolate. She stirs in heavy cream, milk, and a drizzle of corn syrup to create a rich and creamy hot chocolate with an intense flavor. Spoon some of Nicole's marshmallow cream on top for the final touch.

HOT CHOCOLATE

1 cup heavy cream

3 cups whole milk

4 tablespoons light corn syrup

2 cinnamon quills

4 1/2 ounces Valrhona Equatoriale Chocolate, chopped

In a saucepan over medium-low heat, combine the cream, milk, corn syrup, and cinnamon quills and bring to a simmer. Remove from the heat and add the chocolate. Stir until the chocolate is completely melted. Pour into demitasse cups and serve immediately topped with marshmallow.

MAKES 8 DEMITASSE SERVINGS

Marshmallow Cream

4 cups sugar

2 tablespoons light corn syrup

4 tablespoons powdered gelatin

1/2 cup egg whites (from about 3 large eggs)

Sanitize a 1-quart glass jar by submerging it in boiling water for at least 20 minutes. Remove and handle the jar only with tongs and pot holders.

To make the marshmallow cream, in a sauce-pan over medium-low heat, combine the sugar, 1 3/4 cups water, and the corn syrup and heat until temperature reaches 260°F on a candy thermometer. While the sugar is heating, in a small bowl, stir together the gelatin and 1 1/4 cups water. Once the gelatin has absorbed the water, microwave on low power at 15-second intervals. When sugar has reached the proper temperature, add the melted gelatin. Also, while sugar is heating, with an electric stand mixer on high speed, whip the egg whites until stiff.

When whites are stiff, reduce the mixer speed to slow and slowly pour the hot sugar mixture into the whites in a fine stream close to the edge of the bowl. Try to avoid pouring the sugar into the whisk itself. Allow to cool slightly and pour into the sanitized jar. Let stand at room temperature until fully cooled. Refrigerated and unopened, marshmallow cream will last for 3 to 4 months; once opened it will keep for 1 to 2 weeks.

MAKES 4 CUPS

In very cold climates it is the thoughtful custom of some hostesses to have a cup of hot chocolate or bouillon offered each departing guest. This is an especially welcome attention to those who have a long drive home.

EMILY POST, *ETIQUETTE FOR A SIT-DOWN SUPPER*

S'mores Hot Chocolate with Graham Crackers

Caesar Bradley, Ritz-Carlton Hotel, Philadelphia, Pennsylvania

With the title of Hot Chocolate Sommelier at Philadelphia's Ritz-Carlton Hotel, Caesar Bradley's job is to know the history of chocolate, the flavor profiles of chocolate, and all the combinations of ingredients that can transform everyday hot chocolate into a special occasion. He offers hotel guests a selection from urns of milk, dark, and white hot chocolates with their choice of nearly two dozen garnish options, not to mention alcoholic additions. Each hot chocolate is a customized work of confectionary art, each made to order.

The sommelier insists that graham crackers are the ultimate accompaniment to hot chocolate, and he is particularly proud of his "liquid s'mores," constructed with milk chocolate, whipped cream, and marshmallows and served in a mug rimmed with crumbled graham crackers.

HOT CHOCOLATE

$^1/_2$ cup whole milk

$^1/_2$ cup heavy cream

$^1/_2$ to 2 tablespoons sugar

$2^1/_2$ ounces Valrhona bittersweet chocolate, chopped

Pinch of Mexican cinnamon

Butter to rim the mug

Graham cracker crumbs to rim the mug

1 generous tablespoon whipped cream

1 large marshmallow

1 pinch unsweetened cocoa powder (optional)

In a saucepan over low heat, combine the milk, cream, and sugar and heat until sugar is dissolved. Add the chocolate and cinnamon and whisk constantly until the chocolate is melted. Do not let the mixture come to a boil. Rub butter around the rim of a mug, dip into graham cracker crumbs to coat, and fill the mug with the

CONTINUED

hot chocolate. Place the whipped cream and marshmallow on top and sprinkle with the cocoa powder, if desired. Serve immediately with additional graham crackers on the side.

MAKES 1 SERVING

Graham Crackers

1 cup all-purpose flour

1 1/4 cups whole-wheat flour

3/4 cup firmly packed brown sugar

1 teaspoon baking powder

1/2 teaspoon baking soda

1/2 teaspoon salt

1/4 teaspoon ground cinnamon

1/2 cup cold unsalted butter, cut into small pieces

4 tablespoons honey

1 tablespoon molasses

1 teaspoon pure vanilla extract

Preheat the oven to 350°F. In the bowl of an electric stand mixer, mix together the flours, brown sugar, baking powder, baking soda, salt, and cinnamon. Add the butter and mix until the mixture resembles coarse meal. Add the honey, molasses, 1/4 cup cold water, and the vanilla. Mix until the dough comes together in a ball, adding up to an additional 1/4 cup of water if needed. Place half the dough on an ungreased baking sheet and flatten with a rolling pin to cover almost the entire baking sheet, leaving 1 inch around the edges and dusting the dough with flour if necessary to keep it from sticking to the rolling pin. Repeat this process with another cookie sheet and the remaining dough. Score the dough with a knife into 2-inch squares, and prick several holes in each cracker with a fork. Bake until brown, about 13 minutes. Remove from the oven and let the crackers cool on the baking sheet.

MAKES 48 CRACKERS

Warm Bittersweet Chocolate Custard with Toasted Chile Pepper Marshmallows and Cheese Arepa

Rick Griggs, Abacus Restaurant, Dallas, Texas

It was in Friendswood, Texas, that young Rick Griggs first learned to bake fruit pies and make hot chocolate at his grandmother's side. Rick's thematic hot chocolate straddles the line between whimsical and classic, integrating southern hemisphere traditions with his signature interpretive style. Heavy cream and egg yolks turn the warm chocolate into an eat-it-with-a-spoon custard that's topped with Mexican pasilla and cayenne-spiced marshmallows toasted to release their aromatics. Griddled corn cakes, or *arepas,* are the "daily bread" for most families in Venezuela and Colombia. Here they are layered with ripened, semihard farmer's cheese, providing a rustic accompaniment to the chocolate dish.

CUSTARD HOT CHOCOLATE

6 ounces bittersweet chocolate

2 cups whole milk

2 cups heavy cream

1 cinnamon quill

1 star anise

1/2 vanilla bean, seeds removed

1/2 cup firmly packed light brown sugar

4 large egg yolks

6 black peppercorns

In a dry bowl set over a pan of simmering water, melt the chocolate, stirring frequently. Meanwhile, in a saucepan over medium-low heat, combine the milk, cream, cinnamon quill, star anise, and scraped vanilla bean and bring to a low boil. Remove from the heat and allow the mixture to steep for 15 minutes. Once it has steeped, add about 1 cup of the milk mixture to the melted chocolate and stir until smooth. Set aside. Add half of the brown sugar to the milk mixture and stir to dissolve. In a separate bowl, combine the egg yolks with the remaining brown sugar and whisk until incorporated. Temper

CONTINUED

some of the warm cream into the egg yolks by whisking while pouring a small amount of cream into the yolks, then pouring the yolk mixture back into the cream. Add all of the ingredients, including the chocolate, into the cream. Stir constantly over low heat until the mixture coats the back of a spoon. Pour immediately into small cups and add lots of small cubed marshmallows. Place filled cups 6 inches under a broiler, watching very closely, for 30 seconds or until marshmallows caramelize and turn golden brown on top. Serve with arepas on the side.

MAKES 8 DEMITASSE SERVINGS

Chile Pepper Marshmallows

3 tablespoons powdered gelatin

3 cups sugar

1 1/4 cups light corn syrup

1/4 teaspoon salt

2 teaspoons pure vanilla extract

4 tablespoons pasilla chile powder

1/2 teaspoon ground cayenne pepper

Confectioners' sugar for dusting (optional)

In a small bowl, sprinkle the gelatin over 3/4 cup water. Set aside and allow gelatin to soften. In a saucepan over high heat, combine 3/4 water with the sugar, corn syrup, and salt. Bring to a boil and cook until the mixture reaches 240°F on a candy thermometer. In the bowl of an electric stand mixer, whip the gelatin mixture on low speed until fully incorporated. Carefully pour the hot sugar mixture into the gelatin mixture. Increase the speed to high, add the vanilla, and whip until cool, about 10 minutes. Add the chile powder and cayenne and stir to combine. Lightly coat a half-sheet pan with nonstick cooking spray and spread the mixture into the pan with a spatula. Alternatively, use a pastry bag to pipe the mixture into desired shapes on a sheet of parchment paper dusted with confectioners' sugar. Let cool to room temperature, then remove from pan and cut into 1/2-inch squares. Dust with confectioners' sugar.

Arepas with White Farmer's Cheese

1 cup masarepa (instant cornmeal mix)
1/2 teaspoon salt, plus a pinch
Pinch of freshly ground black pepper
1 tablespoon unsalted butter
12 ounces white farmer's cheese, sliced

In a bowl, combine 1 cup warm water with the masarepa, salt, and pepper to form a stiff dough. If it seems too dry, add a little more water. Divide the dough into 4 pieces. Shape each piece into a ball, and then, using your dampened hands, flatten each ball onto a piece of plastic wrap or waxed paper into the shape of a pancake. Heat a nonstick pan over medium heat and cook the arepas 1 at a time for 3 to 5 minutes on each side. The dough may stick to the pan for a minute, but once the arepa starts cooking it will release. Flip over and cook on the other side. Rub each arepa with butter and sprinkle with a pinch of salt. Top with the cheese and serve while still warm.

MAKES 8 CORNCAKES

Reception Hot Chocolate with Coconut Marshmallow

Ann Amernick, Palena, Washington, D.C.

Reserved for formal gatherings, a "reception" hot chocolate came into favor in the 1920s, when nonalcoholic refreshments were intended to replace champagne punches and cider bowls during the "noble experiment" called Prohibition.

Ann Amernick served as assistant to White House pastry chef Roland Mesnier in the Carter years, so she is a practiced hand at stirring the pot. Jimmy Carter never served hot chocolate at White House receptions, but, as a student of culinary history, Ann was inspired to reinvent the drink she imagines might have been served at the "dry" gatherings hosted by Calvin Coolidge, a drink that warms from the inside out.

Aerated confections with a chewy texture have always been exceptionally popular with children, and it's a particularly American conceit to add marshmallows to a steaming cup of liquid chocolate. In Ann's recipe, the distinctive taste of toasted coconut with the creaminess of soft marshmallows makes the hot chocolate extra special.

HOT CHOCOLATE

2 ounces semisweet chocolate (62 percent cacao), chopped

2 ounces bittersweet chocolate (70 percent cacao), chopped

3 tablespoons sugar

1/2 cup heavy cream

3 cups whole milk

Combine the chocolates and 2/3 cup water in a glass or plastic 1-quart bowl. Heat in the microwave at high power for 30 seconds. Remove from the microwave and stir. Continue heating for 10 seconds at a time, stirring after each interval, until the chocolate is melted and the mixture

CONTINUED

is smooth and creamy. Allow to cool slightly. Meanwhile, in a bowl, beat the cream with a whisk until it forms stiff peaks. Fold the whipped cream into the cooled chocolate mixture until combined. In a saucepan over medium heat, heat the milk until very hot but not boiling. Spoon about 1 1/2 cup of the chocolate-cream mixture into a mug, pour 1/4 cup hot milk on top, and top with a coconut marshmallow. Serve immediately.

MAKES 8 DEMITASSE SERVINGS

Coconut Marshmallows

4 cups whole milk
3 cups dry coconut
1 cup confectioners' sugar
Seeds of 1 vanilla bean
3 tablespoons gelatin
2 cups granulated sugar
1/2 cup light corn syrup
3 large egg whites
1 teaspoon pure vanilla extract

To make the toasted coconut, heat the milk in a saucepan over medium heat to just under a boil. Place the coconut in a bowl, pour the milk over it, and let soak for 30 minutes. Strain and press the liquid out of the coconut until it is completely dry. Spread it on a parchment-lined baking sheet and, using a spatula, mix with the confectioners' sugar and the seeds scraped from 1 vanilla bean. Toast in a 300°F oven for 8 minutes. With a spatula, turn the coconut over, stirring it around so that it toasts evenly. Return to the oven and continue toasting 5 minutes. Repeat the process, turning the coconut and toasting it in 5-minute intervals, until it is dry and evenly toasted. Allow to cool.

To make the marshmallows, combine the gelatin with 1/4 cup cold water, stir to mix, and set aside for the gelatin to soften. In a saucepan over medium-high heat, combine the sugar, corn syrup, and 1/2 cup water. Bring to a boil, washing down the sides of the pan with a brush dipped in cold water. Continue cooking until the mixture registers 240°F on a candy thermometer. Meanwhile, place the egg whites in the bowl of an electric stand mixer fitted with a whisk attachment, and beat until soft peaks form. Place the bowl with the gelatin mixture over a bowl of hot water to gently heat, and stir to dissolve. The gelatin mixture and egg whites should be ready when the syrup reaches 240°F.

Stir the melted gelatin into the egg whites, then turn the stand mixer on low and slowly add the sugar, cornsyrup, and water mixture and add the vanilla. Increase mixer speed to high and beat until the mixture is thick and cooled. Spread the mixture into the prepared pan and sprinkle with a little less than half of the toasted coconut. Set aside for several hours or overnight at room temperature, then turn the marshmallow out of the pan and dust with the most of the remaining toasted coconut. When the marshmallows are cut into squares they can be rolled in what's left of the coconut.

MAKES 24 MARSHMALLOWS

Maple Milk Chocolate Pudding/Dipping Sauce with Crispy Bacon Lardons

Katrina Markoff, Vosges Haut-Chocolat, Chicago, New York, Las Vegas

After attending Le Cordon Bleu in Paris, Katrina Markoff served an apprenticeship with the pastry chef at the Hôtel de Crillon. "Every morning, it was my duty as *stagiere* [apprentice] to make the morning brew of hot chocolate, infused with orange peels, cinnamon, and Tahitian vanilla bean, thick with Valrhona chocolate and cream," says Katrina. "I was in hot chocolate heaven!"

Her experiences cooking in France, Spain, and Thailand have inspired her unconventional chocolate making and one-of-a-kind hot chocolates, including a peculiar maple syrup hot chocolate served with crisp bacon for dipping (Katrina recommends hickory- and juniper-smoked bacon from Nodine's Smokehouse in Goshen, Connecticut). The recipe is an expression of Katrina's "love affair with salt and sugar—one taste craves the next."

The etiquette is simple: Plunge the bacon into the pudding and take a bite. The front of the tongue tastes the sweetness of maple and chocolate, the front edges taste the salt of the bacon. It's a sensory moment of yin/yang, two opposite characters in a dizzying counterbalance and a lingering moment that results in complete pleasure.

1 cup heavy cream

4 ounces milk chocolate, chopped

1 10-ounce slab of hickory-smoked bacon

1 tablespoon unsalted butter, at room temperature

1 tablespoon organic Grade A maple syrup, plus more for garnish

In a saucepan over medium-low heat, bring the cream to a boil. Remove from heat and pour over the chocolate in a heatproof bowl. Cover with plastic wrap and let sit for 5 minutes. Cut the bacon into 1-inch-wide strips. Heat a skillet over medium-high heat and cook the bacon until golden brown and crispy. Drain the bacon on paper towels. Stir the cream and chocolate mixture slowly to combine. Add the butter and maple syrup and stir until the butter is melted and the ingredients are thoroughly combined. Pour the chocolate mixture into tall vodka glasses, drizzle with extra maple syrup. Serve immediately with a piece of bacon arranged across the top of the glass.

MAKES 2 DEMITASSE SERVINGS

GRAHAM CRACKERS

These flat, crisp crackers, made with whole wheat flour and sweetened with honey, were created in the 1830s by clergyman and nutrition advocate Sylvester Graham, who promoted his recipe as a health food (he refused to wash them down with anything stronger than water himself). Nabisco still produces Graham crackers with perforations that allow you to break each one into four sticks—perfect for dunking into hot chocolate.

Whipped Cream Menu

The contrast between cool, lightly sweetened whipped cream and warm, dark hot chocolate adds an extra dimension and furnishes a measure of elegance to the drink. The fluffy cloud, of course, is nothing more than heavy cream beaten until air bubbles are incorporated, so please don't settle for imitation products or, heaven forbid, "whipped topping" out of a pressurized can. The difference in texture and flavor is dramatic. Real whipped cream is so luscious it almost begs to be eaten all by itself.

To make whipped cream, first ensure that the cream is very cold, straight from the refrigerator. Chilling the bowl and whisk will also help the cream achieve the maximum volume possible. Whip the cold cream with a rotary egg beater or an electric mixer at moderate speed until the cream is slightly thickened. When it reaches this stage, add the sugar or other flavoring ingredients. Continue whipping until the cream forms distinct mounds that hold their shape. Don't whip beyond the soft-peak stage, because the cream will get stiff and curdle.

To sweeten whipped cream, always use confectioners' sugar instead of granulated sugar, which can result in a gritty texture. Possible flavorings include almost any type of flavoring extract, chocolate, coffee, citrus zest, and spices, as well as bourbon, rum, brandy, and other liqueurs. As the whipped cream melts into the hot chocolate, the flavors will soften and marry into a more savory drink.

Note: Whipped cream made with good-quality cream should last for 24 hours covered in the refrigerator. To stabilize whipped cream and prevent it from separating, melt a marshmallow and incorporate it into the whipped cream near the end of the whipping time.

Basic Whipped Cream

1 cup heavy cream
2 tablespoons confectioners' sugar
1/2 teaspoon pure vanilla extract

In a mixing bowl, whip the cream until the cream is slightly thickened. Add the remaining ingredients and continue whipping until cream holds its shape. Spoon on top of hot chocolate.

MAKES 2 CUPS

Use the same method for each of the following recipes.

Cayenne Whipped Cream

1 cup heavy cream
2 tablespoons confectioners' sugar
1/2 teaspoon pure vanilla extract
Pinch of ground cayenne pepper

Chocolate Whipped Cream

1 cup heavy cream
2 tablespoons confectioners' sugar
1/2 teaspoon pure vanilla extract
1/4 cup unsweetened Dutch-process cocoa powder

Cinnamon Whipped Cream

1 cup heavy cream
2 tablespoons confectioners' sugar
1/2 teaspoon pure vanilla extract
1 teaspoon ground cinnamon

Bourbon Whipped Cream

1 cup heavy cream
1 tablespoon confectioners' sugar
1/2 teaspoons pure vanilla extract
2 teaspoons bourbon

Ginger Whipped Cream

1 cup heavy cream
2 tablespoons confectioners' sugar
1 teaspoon ground ginger

Resources

Chocolate

El Rey America
P.O. Box 853
Fredericksburg, TX 78624
(800) EL-REY-99 or (830) 997-2200
www.elreychocolate.com

Scharffen Berger Chocolate Maker
914 Heinz Avenue
Berkeley, CA 94710
(800) 930-4528 or (510) 981-4050
www.scharffenberger.com

E. Guittard
10 Guittard Road
P.O. Box 4308
Burlingame, CA 94010
(800) 468-2462 or (650) 697-4427
www.eguittard.com

Barry Callebaut USA
1500 Suckle Highway
Pennsauken, NJ 08110
(800) 774-9131 or (856) 663-2260
www.chocosphere.com

Valrhona USA
1901 Avenue of the Stars, Suite 1800
Los Angeles, CA 90067
(310) 277-0441
www.chocosphere.com

Omanhene Cocoa Bean Company
P.O. Box 22
Milwaukee, WI 53201
(800) 588-2462 or (414) 332-6252
www.omanhene.com

Michel Cluizel
c/o Vintage Chocolates
1 Atalanta Plaza
Elizabeth, NJ 07206
(800) 207-7058 or (908) 354-9304
www.echocolates.com

Mexican Chocolate

Chocolate Ibarra
Chocolateria de Jalisco
Avenue Mariano Otero No. 1420, Col.
Verde Valle C.P. 44510
Guadalajara, Jalisco, Mexico
www.mexgrocer.com

Moctezuma
Boulevard Industrial No. 301, Col.
Eduardo Ruiz
Uruapan, Michoacán, Mexico
www.mexgrocer.com

La Popular
Fab. De Chocolate La Popular,
S.A. DE C.V.
Aramberri Ote. No. 112, Centro 64000
Monterrey, Nuevo Leon, Mexico
www.melissaguerra.com

Shaved Chocolate

Jacques Torres Chocolate
66 Water Street
Brooklyn, NY 11201
(718) 875-9772
www.newyorkfirst.com
Classic Hot Chocolate, Wicked Hot Chocolate

MarieBelle
484 Broome Street
New York, NY 10013
(212) 925-6999
www.newyorkfirst.com
Aztec, Dark, Mocha, Spicy

Vosges Haut-Chocolate
520 N. Michigan Avenue
Chicago, IL 60611
(312) 644-9450
www.vosgeschocolate.com
Aztec Elixir, La Parisienne, Bianca

Cioccolateria Slitti
Via Francesca Sud
1268-51015 Monsummano Terme
Pistoia, Tuscany, Italy
www.chocosphere.com
Traditional, Cinnamon, Chilli

Scharffen Berger
914 Heinz Avenue
Berkeley, CA 94710
(800) 930-4528 or (510) 981-4050
www.scharffenberger.com
Drinking Chocolate

Charbonnel et Walker
28 Old Bond Street
London W1S 4BT
www.charbonnel.co.uk
Chocolat Charbonnel

Browne's Hand Made Chocolates
Throwleigh, Devon EX20 2HX
www.brownes.co.uk
Luxurious Drinking Chocolate

Chocolat Bonnat
Colette and Sons, Official Retailer
6624 Springpark Avenue, Suite 5
Los Angeles, CA 90056
(310) 417-8977
www.chocolatetradingco.com
Dark Chocolate Flakes
Chocolate Flakes with Honey and Lime

Lake Champlain Chocolates
750 Pine Street
(800) 465-5909 or (802) 864-1808
Burlington, VT 05401
www.lakechamplainchocolates.com
"Old World" Selection

La Maison du Chocolat
Les Guilleraies, 41–43 rue Paul Lescop
92000 Nanterre, Paris France
www.lamaisonduchocolat.com
Tasse de Chocolat

Valor Chocolates
2770 N.W. 24th Street
Miami, FL 33142
(305) 634-7711
www.chocosphere.com
Valor Cao Hot Chocolate Powder

Fran's Chocolates, Ltd.
1300 East Pike Street
Seattle, WA 98122
(800) 422-FRAN or (206) 322-0233
www.franschocolates.com
Shaved Chocolate

Schokinag North America, Inc.
5301 Office Park Drive, Suite 200
Bakersfield, CA 93309
(800) 807-2465
www.drinkyourchocolate.com
European Drinking Chocolate

Dagoba Organic Chocolate
P.O. Box 5330
Central Point, OR 97502
(800) 393-6075 or (541) 664-9030
www.dagobachocolate.com
Authentic Hot Chocolate, Xocolatl Hot Chocolate

Green & Black's
2 Valentine Place
London SE1 8QH
www.chocosphere.com
Organic Hot Chocolate

Dolfin
Chaussée de Tubize, 59
1440 Wauthier Braine
Belgium
www.chocosphere.com
Copeaux de Chocolat

Fauchon
35-02 Borden Avenue
Long Island City, NY 11101
(866) 784-7001
www.fauchon.com
Hot Chocolate

Xocoatl
107-B Juan Largo Lane
Taos, NM 87571
(505) 751-7549
www.chocolatecartel.com
Mayan Hot Chocolate Mix

Dufflet Bakery
41 Dovercourt Road
Toronto, Ontario M6J 3C2
(866) 238-0899 or (416) 536-9640
www.dufflet.com
Luxury Hot Chocolate

Café Tasse
1, Avenue Reine Astrid
1440 Wauthier-Braine
Belgium
www.chocosphere.com

L.A. Burdick
P.O. Box 593
Walpole, NH 03608
(800) 229-2419
www.laburdick.com
Hot Chocolate for Home

Enric Rovira
Sant Geroni 17
08296 Castellbell i el Vilar
Barcelona, Spain
www.seventypercent.com
Chocolate a la Taza

Williams-Sonoma
3250 Van Ness Avenue
San Francisco, CA 94109
(877) 812-6235 or (415) 421-7900
www.williams-sonoma.com
Hot Chocolate, Peppermint Hot Chocolate

Cocoa Powders

Fairly Traded Organic
Hot Cocoa Mix
Equal Exchange, Inc.
50 United Drive
West Bridgewater, MA 02379
(774) 776-7400
www.equalexchange.com

Scharffen Berger
914 Heinz Avenue
Berkeley, CA 94710
(800) 930-4528 or (510) 981-4050
www.scharffenberger.com
Natural Cocoa Powder

Ghirardelli Chocolate Co.
1111 139th Avenue
San Leandro, CA 94578
(800) 877-9338
www.ghirardelli.com
*Double Chocolate, Chocolate Mocha,
Chocolate Hazelnut, White Mocha*

Mocafe
P.O. Box 6373
Laguna Niguel, CA 92607
(888) 662-2334
www.mocafe.net
Mexican Spiced Cocoa Azteca D'Oro

Max Brenner Chocolat
447 Oxford Street
Paddington, Australia
www.chocosphere.com
Hot Chocolate Powder

Omanhene Cocoa Bean Company
P.O. Box 22
Milwaukee, WI 53201
(800) 588-2462 or (414) 332-6252
www.omanhene.com
Hot Cocoa Mix

Droste Nederland B.V.
P.O. Box 5
NL 8170 AA Vaassen
The Netherlands
www.cardullos.com
Dutch Cocoa Powder

About the Author

Michael Turback was trained as a restaurateur at the Cornell University School of Hotel Administration. For nearly three decades, he operated Turback's of Ithaca, a restaurant whose mission was to combine inventiveness, passionate cooking with local ingredients, and the novel concept of an all–New York State wine list. He is a founding partner in two electronic commerce ventures, The New York First Company, an online department store, and History Company, an online catalog of historic reproductions. As an author, Mr. Turback has written about his hometown's invention of the ice cream sundae and commemorated the centennial of the banana split. His previous work for Ten Speed Press, *Greetings from the Finger Lakes: A Food and Wine Lover's Companion,* is a celebration of the region's achievements in winemaking, artisan farming, and culinary invention. He lives in the enlightened city of Ithaca, New York, with his wife, Juliet.

Index

A

Allspice, 17
Almond oil/extract, 69, 117–18
Amernick, Ann, 130–33
Angelina (Paris, France), 35
Anise, star, 40, 127–28
Antioxidants, 12
Antonorsi, Michael, 21–22
Arepas with White Farmers Cheese, 129
Arestrel, Madame d', 10
Artisan du Chocolat, L' (London, England), 32
Art of Chocolate, The (New York, NY), 44
Auberge du Cochon Rouge, L' (Ithaca, NY), 82–83

B

Bachot, Joseph, 4
Bacon Lardons, Crispy, 134–35
Barry Callebaut USA, 138
Bay leaves, 52–53, 79–80

Beer, 65
Béguin, Victor, 50–51
Beignets, Cherry-Chocolate Ricotta, 109
Bigelow, Fran, 54–55
Black Bottom Hot Chocolate, 100–101
Black pepper, 38–39, 115–16
Boston Beer Company, 65
Bourbon Whipped Cream, 137
Bradley, Caesar, 125–26
Brandy, 69, 81
Brillat-Savarin, Jean-Anthelme, 10, 51, 57
British Spectator, 11
Browne's Hand Made Chocolates (Throwleigh, England), 140
Brown Russian, 79–80
Bruce, Stephen, 87–88
Budd, Dan, 79–80
Burdick, L. A., 142
Buttered Rum, Hot Chocolate, 66–67

C

Cacao nibs, 111
Café Cacao (Berkeley, CA), 110–11
Café Mozart (Vienna, Austria), 27
Café-Style Hot Chocolate, 45
Café Tasse (Wauthier-Braine, Belgium), 141
Caffè Florian (Venice, Italy), 31
Cajeta (dulce de leche), 107
Campbell, Scott, 59
Canadian whiskey, 75
Canela, 90–91, 117–18
Caramel, 54–55, 56–57
Cardamom, 21–22
Carême, Antonin, 63
Carob, 103–4
Carter, Jimmy, 130
Catalan Cloud, 112–13
Cayenne pepper, 17, 21–22, 82–83, 115–16, 128–29, 137
Ceiba (Washington, D.C.), 117–18

Chang, Joanne, 92–93

Charbonnel et Walker (London, England), 140

Cheese, 21–22, 66–67, 109, 129

Cherry-Chocolate Ricotta Beignet, 109

Chesterton, G. K., 3

Chestnut Hot Chocolate, 81

Chiles, 21–22, 23–24, 112–13,128–29,

Chile powder, 65

Chinese Five-Spice Hot Chocolate, 40

Chocolat Bonnat (Los Angeles, CA), 140

Chocolate a la Taza, 30

Chocolate Arts (Vancouver, B.C., Canada), 58

Chocolate Bar (New York, NY), 60

Chocolate Caliente para Agasajos, 23–24

Chocolate chips, 109, 120–21

Chocolate Ibarra (Guadalajara, Mexico), 139

Chocolate Irish Coffee, 84

Chocolatería San Ginés (Madrid, Spain), 30

Chocolate Whipped Cream, 137

Chocolat l'Africain, Le, 35

Chokladkoppen (Stockholm, Sweden), 28

Christopher Elbow Artisanal Chocolate (Kansas City, MO), 40

Chuao Chocolatier (Encinitas, CA), 21–22

Churros, Cinnamon-Dusted, 118

Cinnamon, 40, 66–67, 72–74, 79–80, 81, 82–83, 90–91, 115–116, 118, 122, 125–26, 127–28, 137

Cioccolateria Slitti (Pistoia, Italy), 139

Cioccolato Caldo, 31

Citizen Cake (San Francisco, CA), 103–4

Citrus Hot Chocolate, 44

Cloves, 16, 40, 43, 79–80, 82–83

Cluizel, Michel, 10, 139

Cocoa powder, 3–4

Cocoa West Chocolatier (Bowen Island, Canada), 43

Coconut/coconut milk, 72–74, 132–33

Coffee, 68, 81, 90–91

Coffee liqueur, 114

Cointreau, 82–83

Coleman, Gerard, 32

Cookies

Nibby, 111

Tahini, 74

Tuile, 121

Coston, Patrick, 44

Crackers, Graham, 126, 135

Crème de menthe, 84

Cucharamama (Hoboken, NJ), 23–24

Custard, Warm Bittersweet Chocolate, 127–28

Cuthbert, Kimberly Davis, 56–57

D

Dagoba Organic Chocolate (Central Point, OR), 141

Da Ponte, Lorenzo, 55

Deer Valley Resort (Park City, UT), 114–16

Denny, Patty, 69

Diaz del Castillo, Bernal, 22

Dipping Sauce, Maple Milk Chocolate, 134–35

Dolfin (Wauthier-Braine, Belgium), 141

Double Chocolate Hot Chocolate, 42

Droste Nederland B.V. (Vaassen, Netherlands), 143

Dufflet Bakery (Toronto, Canada), 71, 141

Dulce de Leche, Hot Chocolate, 107

E

Eggnog, Hot Chocolate, 96–97

Elbow, Christopher, 40

El Rey America (Fredericksburg, TX), 138

El Rey chocolate, in Fatale Chocolate, 112–13

Espuma, 18, 72–74

Extraordinary Desserts (San Diego, CA), 107–9

F

Fairly Traded Organic Hot Cocoa Mix (West Bridge-water, MA), 142

Farallon (San Francisco, CA), 42

Farmers Cheese, 21–22, 129

Fatale Chocolate with Catalan Cloud, 112–13

Fauchon (Long Island City, NY), 141

Falkner, Elizabeth, 103–4

Fennel seed, 40

Flatt, Letty Halloran, 114–16

Flour Bakery (Boston, MA), 92–93

Fondue, Mexican Hot Chocolate, 90–91

Fran's Chocolates (Seattle, WA), 54–55, 140

Frangelico, 70–71, 81

Frrrozen Hot Chocolate, 87–88

Fudge, 100–101

G

Gabrielle (New Orleans, LA), 68

Gand, Gale, 90–91

Gayer-Nicholson, Michelle, 66–67

General Foods, 113

Ghirardelli Chocolate Co. (San Francisco, CA), 84, 142

Ginger, 56–57, 79–80, 137

Goldsmith, Hedy, 98–99

Graham, Sylvester, 135

Graham Crackers, 126, 135

Grand Finale Hot Chocolate with Marshmallow Cream, 122–23

Grand Marnier, 44, 82–83

Grand Restaurant Schuh (Interlaken, Switzerland), 33

Green & Black's (London, England), 141

Grishman, Linda, 75

Guas, David, 117–18

Guittard, E., 138

Guittard "Etienne" chocolate, 75

H

Habañero chiles, 112–13

Hanahato sake, 72–74

Hasson, Julie, 94

Hazelnuts, 70–71

Heisse Schokolade mit Mélange, 33

Heisse Schokolade mit Schlagobers, 27

Hellfire Hot Chocolate, 17

Hershey Company, 88, 93

Het Choklad Vit, 28

Hook, Greg, 58

Hot Butterscotch with White Chocolate, 94

HOTCHOCOLATE (Chicago, IL), 100–101

Hot Chocolate à l'Orange, 82–83

Hot Chocolate Buttered Rum, 66–67

Hot! Chocolate Cookies, 115–16

Hot Chocolate Dulce de Leche with Cherry-Chocolate Ricotta Beignet, 107–9

Hot Chocolate Eggnog, 96–97

Hot Chocolate Nightcap Tequila, 75

Hot Chocolate Reviver, 69

Hot Chocolate with Tuile Cookies, 120–21

Howard, Ethan, 48

Hungarian Heat, 43

I

Ice cream, 95

Iced hot chocolates, 87–88, 95, 110–11

Irish Coffee, Chocolate, 84

J

Jack Daniel's, 77

Jackson, Shirley, 101

Jacques Torres Chocolate (Brooklyn, NY), 139

Jefferson, Thomas, 5

Jesuit monasteries, 37

JS Bonbons (Toronto, Canada), 38–39

K

Kahlua, 77

Key Lime Pie Hot Chocolate, 98–99

Kingsbury, Robert, 47

Kingsbury Chocolates (Alexandria, VA), 47
Knapp, Arthur W., 39
Knives, 7
Krasne, Karen, 107–9

L

La Bonne Table (Peterborough, NH), 50–51
La Bonne Table Hot Chocolate, 50–51
Lake Champlain Chocolates (Burlington, VT), 140
La Maison du Chocolat (Paris, France), 140
La Popular (Monterrey, Mexico), 139
Lavender-Pistachio Hot Chocolate, 47
Lee, Chang Yong, 12
Lemery, Louis, 8
Lemons, 112–13
Lewis, Matt, 60
Lieberman, Maribel, 76
Life-in-a-Cup Hot Chocolate, 19
Limes, 98–99
Linda Grishman Chocolates (Burlington, VT), 75
Louis XV, 11
Luchetti, Emily, 42

M

Macias, Ivan and Gus, 77
Malted Hot Chocolate, 60
Mann, Thomas, 116
Maple syrup, 75, 134–35
Maria Theresa (Queen of Spain), 15
Marie Antoinette, 53
MarieBelle (New York, NY), 76, 139
MarieBelle "Aztec" Hot Chocolate, 76
Mariposa Hot Chocolate with Hot! Chocolate Cookies, 114–16
Markoff, Katrina, 134–35
Marshmallow(s), 59, 122–23, 125–26, 128–29, 132–33
Martini House (St. Helena, CA), 48
Masa, 19
Masarepa, 129
Mascarpone Cream, 66–67
Matcha Hot Chocolate, 58
Mautone, Nick, 81
Max Brenner Chocolat (Paddington, Australia), 143
Mélange, Heisse Schokolade mit, 33
Merle, Etienne, 82
Mesnier, Roland, 130
Metric conversions/ equivalents, 6

Mexican chocolate, 3, 139
Mexican Hot Chocolate Fondue, 90–91
Meyers dark rum, 77
Midnight Cowboy, 77
Mint, 79–80
Mixes, hot chocolate, 3, 142
Mocafe (Laguna Niguel, CA), 143
Mocha
Iced Chocolate Mocha, 110
Mocha Voodoo, 68
Moctezuma (Uruapan, Mexico), 139
Mogridge, Joanne, 43
Molinillos, 9
Montezuma, 3, 11, 87
Morley, Christopher, 97
Myers, Michelle, 112–13

N

Nash, Ogden, 63
NEMO (Miami Beach, FL), 98–99
"New" Mexican Hot Chocolate with Cinnamon-Dusted Churros, 117–18
Nibby Cookies, 111
Nueva Bogotá Hot Chocolate, 21–22
Nutella Hot/Frozen Hot Chocolate, 95
Nutmeg, 66–67, 79–80, 82–83

O

Omanhene chocolate, 35
Omanhene Cocoa Bean Co.
   (Milwaukee, WI),
   138, 143
Oranges, 28, 44, 66–67,
   82–83, 112–13
Oren, Arnon, 110–11
Ortuzar, Sisha, 52–53

P

Palena (Washington, D.C.),
   130–33
Panela/panocha/papelon, 21
Paprika, 43
Paris Crêperie (Brookline,
   MA), 95
Partridge, Tim, 120–21
Patisserie Bleu (Nashua,
   NH), 45
Peanut Butter Hot Chocolate,
   59
Pearl Bakery (Portland, OR),
   96–97
Peppermint Hot Chocolate, 48
Peppers. See Black pepper;
   Cayenne pepper; Chiles
Pepys, Samuel, 71
Perdix (Boston, MA), 120–21
Pessoa, Fernando, 83
Pilonzillo, 21
Pistachio-Lavender Hot
   Chocolate, 47
Pompadour, Madame de, 11

Posey, Lee, 96–97
Post, Emily, 123
Prescott, William Hickling, 24
Presilla, Maricel, 23–24
Pressinger, Jacqui, 45
Prime 112 (Miami Beach, FL),
   98–99
Proust, Marcel, 86
Pudding, Maple Milk
   Chocolate, 134–35
Pungent Spice-Infused Hot
   Chocolate, 16
Purdy, Jan, 19

R

Raisins, chocolate-covered,
   103–4
Reception Hot Chocolate with
   Coconut Marshmallow,
   130–33
Resources, 138–43
Ricotta Beignet, Cherry-
   Chocolate, 109
Ritz-Carlton Hotel
   (Philadelphia, PA), 125–26
Roasted Hazelnut Hot
   Chocolate, 70–71
Rosebuds, 23–24
Rosenberg, Dufflet, 71
Rovira, Enric, 142
Rum, 66–67, 68, 77, 107

S

Saffron, 23–24
Sake-Wasabi Hot Chocolate
   with Tahini Cookies, 72–74
Samuel Adams Adult Hot
   Chocolate, 65
Scales, 6
Scharffenberger, John, 49
Scharffen Berger Chocolate
   (Berkeley, CA), 49,
   110–11, 138, 140, 142
Scharffen Berger Hot
   Chocolate, 49
Schlagobers, Heisse
   Schokolade mit, 27
Schokinag North America, Inc.
   (Bakersfield, CA), 141
Schuh, Christian, 33
Scotch bonnet chiles, 112–13
Scotch whiskey, 94
Segal, Mindy, 100–101
Señor Fred (Sherman Oaks,
   CA), 19
Serendipity 3 (New York,
   NY), 87–88
Sévigné, Marquise de, 26
Shoji Sushi (Miami Beach, FL),
   98–99
Silverston, Chuck, 95
Skating-on-Thin-Ice Hot
   Chocolate, 103–4
S'mores Hot Chocolate with
   Graham Crackers, 125–26

Sona Restaurant (Los Angeles, CA), 112–13
Sonnier, Mary, 68
Sour mash whiskey, 77
Stone, Jenn, 38–39
Stubbe, Henry, 12
Sucanat, 5, 50–51
Sugars, 5
Sushi Samba (New York, NY; Miami, FL; Chicago, IL), 72–74
Sweeteners, 5
Sweet Jazmine's (Berwyn, PA), 56–57
Sweet Spice-Scented Hot Chocolate, 15
Szechuan peppers, 40

T
Tahini Cookies, 74
Tarragon and Black Pepper Hot Chocolate, 38–39
Taste Budds (Red Hook, NY), 79–80
Telluride Truffles (Telluride, CO), 69
Tequila, Hot Chocolate Nightcap, 76

Tong, Vera, 72–74
Tortilla Flats (Santa Fe, NM), 77
Trina Restaurant (Fort Lauderdale, FL), 81
Triple Hot Chocolate Obsession, 92–93
Tru (Chicago, IL), 90–91
Tuile Cookies, 121

V
Valor Chocolates (Miami, FL), 140
Valrhona chocolates, 28, 72–74, 107, 122, 125–26
Valrhona USA, 138
Vanilla ice cream, in Nutella Frozen Hot Chocolate, 95
Vodka, 79–80
Vosges Haut-Chocolat (Chicago, IL; New York, NY; Las Vegas, NV), 134–35, 139

W
Wadsworth, James, 12
Walter Baker & Co., 99
Warm Bittersweet Chocolate Custard with Toasted Chile Pepper Marshmallows and Cheese Arepa, 127–29
Wasabi-Sake Hot Chocolate, 72–74
Whipped cream, 92, 136–37
Whiskey, 75, 77, 84, 94
White chocolate, 28, 58, 92–93
'wichcraft (New York, NY), 52–53
Wilde, Oscar, 91
Williams-Sonoma (San Francisco, CA), 142

X
Xocoatl (Taos, NM), 141

Y
Yogurt, 95